Enough!
Educational Prosperity
For All Learners

Robyne Halevy, Ed.D.
RobyneHalevy.com
Creating Caring Communities

An Ubuntu Press Book
Published by Lightning Source, a subsidiary of
Ingram Press Publishers
Books are available through Ingram Press, and available for order through
Ingram Press Catalogues

Please visit my website at www.robynehalevy.com
Creating Caring Communities
Printed in the United States of America
First Printing: April 2013

ISBN 978-1-62517-092-7

Creating Caring Communities, LLC

Dedication

To my father, David Morris Halevy, who revered education as the ultimate path and that the learning is what really matters.

To my mother, Gloria Louise Halevy, who modeled wholehearted living with relationships as a foundation. Her nickname is Sunshine Glo.

To all my teachers in my circle of learning, my students, colleagues, friends, and family. You have inspired me with your energy, wondering, and insatiable passion for learning.

My father's Voice to me through his letters when I went to college in Fall, 1971.

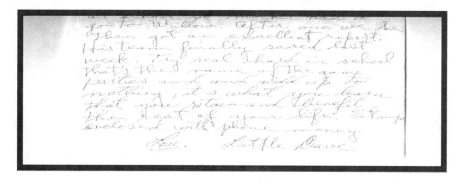

Four Quartets
by T.S. Eliot

We shall not cease from exploration.
And the end of all our exploring
Will be to arrive where we started
And know the place for the very first time.

Chapters

About Enough!

Enough! is about schools, education, and life. We are in an age of massive stimulation, more, more, more, higher, higher, and higher which translates into our obsession for living futuristically, collecting mounds of numerical data, and relegating qualities of humanity as less important. This focus on data creates walls that impede relationships, causes anxiety among educators and learners, and fosters a reductionistic learning environment = poverty of learning.

In addition, our curriculum has been overly processed, just like our foods; it is unhealthy for learners. With minimizing control and customizing learning for each student, we would likely create greater educational health in our schools and communities. By focusing on creating caring communities among our students, families, and educators, we establish a fertile foundation for wholistic learning.

When we honor humanity, view *WE* in a circle, rather than *I* on a ladder of hierarchy, we all feel included, rather than more than, less than. We include rather than exclude. The bounty of learning is limitless!

Enough! is about considering the notion that today, even this moment in time is an opportunity to celebrate our success, achievements, and feel that right now is just right. It is in a place of acceptance where intrinsic motivation occurs. It is in a place of forgiveness of self, that creates *I can* rather than *I can't.*

We live in a world of judgment, of ourselves and others, breeding this feeling of never enough. We can turn this around by honoring each other, learning from and with each other, to create Ubuntu, *I am because we are.*

Enough! is about being mindful and present for the insatiable curiosity all learners have, honoring self content (that which is inside us- our knowledge, feelings and experiences) capitalizing on wondering, searching, finding, and creating.

Rather than always pursuing a time and place different than when and where we are, Enough! embraces learning of today. Rather than nothing seems to be good enough in the moment, Enough! embraces everything as good enough. Acceptance and celebration creates pathways for higher reach.

Enough! is about *Enough*, a double entendre.

We have had
…enough of what is not working.
…enough of poverty of learning in our schools.
…enough of hoards of testing that replaces learning time.
…enough of the anxiety our educators feel every day.
…enough of the anxiety our learners feel every day.
…enough of controlling every move learners make.
…enough of what we are doing in education right now.

and

We have the power to create Enough.
We can learn what is enough for ourselves.
We can learn enough for others.
We can teach our learners to know and be enough for themselves.
We can learn to embrace enough- for today, this hour, this moment, as exactly where we are supposed to be. It may be a moment of achievement, or a moment of struggle, or a moment of silence while we distill all in the world around us.

Enough! is written from the heart and experiences of an observant and seasoned educator. It includes beliefs, ideas, real stories and passion about authentic learning. Although you may not agree with all that is here, it is hoped you *think* and *feel* while reading, reflecting on your own experiences and of those learners you know.

Enough! provides hope, possibility, and prosperity of learning.

Introduction
End Poverty of Learning in our Schools

Our schools have the potential to develop energized, dynamic, eager learners. For several hours a day, we have the opportunity to group learners and build thriving caring communities which cultivates dynamic learning. Our teachers have the opportunity to build relationships with each member in their classroom and to create the environment for students to develop caring, honoring relationships with each other.

Offering opportunities for learners to navigate their learning, nurturing organic conversations, infusing academic with social and emotional capacities would produce capable, confident learners throughout their lives. Children would feel safer in our schools, cared about, cared for, and be able to create their best selves as they develop optimal relationships with each other. The learning capabilities and achievement in these environments would soar!

Instead, we are starving our children of the true essence of learning. There is a poverty of education in our schools today. All too common, students receive a narrow and robotic curriculum. The teacher models something; the students do it. Compliance is the most revered behavior. Less often or nonexistent are organic conversations, student choice in questioning, reading, or allowing students to search inside themselves.

The irony is that even in 1994, my first year as principal, we knew a different direction was needed, and yet, the lists actually have reversed (see Figure 1). What we wanted more of we now have less of; what we wanted less of we now have more of. What we wanted more of drew me into administration. Students today are stifled, smothered in preparing for tests, taking tests, getting monitored like they are on machines. Textbooks are bigger than ever, and more and more, students are not reading them. Teachers are exhausted from the race, the data collection, and looking at test scores of learning—knowing that is not the full measure, nor what matters most.

Our schools are full of contradictions of thinking and action. We say we value Voice in writing, but we continually give prompts for students to respond. How much time do we give to students in developing their own topics? And we wonder why they do not have any ideas when we ask them to write something that is important to them! We say we value student thinking, but we ask them to choose from preselected answers most of the time. We say we value student engagement, but teachers do most of the doing, planning, preparing, and talking in classrooms.

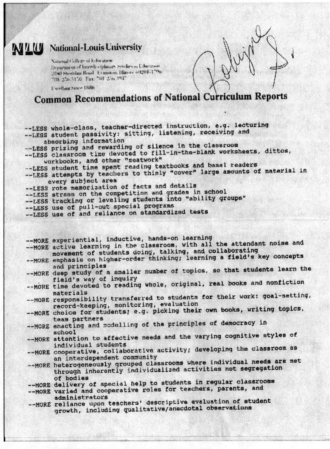

Figure 1, 1994

How can we salvage the education of our children?

Less will be more. When we take less control of students' learning, we empower them to understand their learning processes, invite them to learn to ask their own questions, and seek, discover, and create their own answers. When we design learning communities with members who value each other's contributions, we honor each other as human beings, exactly what we hope for in our global society.

What would it look like if we gave the power of learning to the students? What if we guided students in choosing topics of learning? What if we let the students ask the questions, create the pace for themselves, and determine their homework? What would it look like if the students created the energy of their learning, became inspired, worked together, determined their plan, and took ownership of their learning? What would this look like?

If we ended the hierarchical ranking systems of grades, testing, and numerical intelligent scales, we would be able to honor multiple intelligences. We would honor social and emotional intelligences as the new way to be educated and develop the abilities to navigate a healthy and prosperous life. Developing optimal social and emotional capacities provides us what matters most in life and engenders our ability to grow academically.

We have a new set of Common Core Standards that attempts to create more effective education for our students. The wordings in many cases describe a rich education palette. Unfortunately, so often, our standards become checklists for educators, our "To-Do" lists. Creating student independence is not an activity. It is a way of learning; it is an environment where students become and actually feel independent. Students ask questions, search for resources, find and create answers. Students engage in organic conversations because they become enmeshed in learning. It is a rich flow of reading, writing, and conversation in many contexts. Educators all over the country are "unpacking" the standards and once again, taking charge of the students' learning.

When I peruse my bookshelves and view the book spines of the educators who have inspired me over the years, I can remember what is inside these books. I remember their thoughts, most of all their stories, and how they came to understand and believe what was important to them for school and life experiences. Their stories are weaved with mine. And I wonder why these powerful ideas are still so elusive in our schools.

There are many things we are still doing ineffectively for so many students. I wish we would stop. My dream is for each student to enthusiastically enter their school building every day and feel and think, *I will learn. I will put forth my greatest effort. I know there are people here to guide me. I am safe. I am cared about. I matter. I am worth it.*

What would it take to end the poverty of education for our students? It begins with eliminating the quantitative measurements that rank students and schools against each other. If we truly revere democracy, honor human beings for their abilities, contributions, potentials, and social justice, comparing students to one another hierarchically is counterproductive for our learners.

When we allow customization for our learners, where each and everyone takes the reins of their learning and becomes inspired to reach beyond their perceived capacities of learning. We can create communities of learning where each student's achievement is raised to the highest level possible by helping each other, by believing that one's achievement is a result of working together, helping others achieve their highest potential as well.

We would create *Ubuntu*, a way of life cherished and promoted by Nelson Mandela. "In Africa there is a concept known as *Ubuntu*, the profound sense that we are human only through the humanity of others, that if we are to accomplish anything in the world, it will in equal measure be due to the achievement of others." (Nelson Mandela) *Ubuntu* simply means, "I am because we are." It means, "I need *you* to be me and you need *me* to be you." (Lesser, Tedspeaks)

If we create our schools where *Ubuntu* is our greatest achievement and our greatest pride, our collective achievement would be greater than any one individual. *Ubuntu* is the greatest school in the universe because there is not one student who feels shame in what s/he cannot do. Each learner feels that what s/he can do is an integral part of the whole. Each learner is inspired to work as hard as s/he can because s/he knows his efforts are so important to the whole. The learners know they are an important cog in the wheel and the wheel will stop turning without them.

Every individual is valued and honored in *Ubuntu* School. There is not a hierarchical ranking system among students or staff, because each member feels s/he belongs and is valued for what s/he does and knows differently. Everyone has a Voice and feels s/he can share what matters to him or her. Circle gatherings occur frequently for community building so learning/sharing/ connecting is the center of all doing. Teachers are among the learners.

This book emanates from my deepest core, career, and life as an informal leader, then professional educator and administrator. I listened to what others were saying and doing, all the while forming inside of me an ideal school. One of my favorite children's books, *The Big Orange Splot* by Daniel Manus Pinkwater, colorfully creates the message, "My house is me and I am it and it looks like all my dreams." *Ubuntu* School is me and I am it; it looks like all my dreams.

While I created this ideal school inside of me, I also worked in school environments, studying what worked and what did not. I fought many battles over the years, creating synergy to change things slowly. Now that I am not in a school or system, I can step back and reflect on my true beliefs about education from all those years, form my ideal school I longed to be a learner, offer to my own children, and create to honor our precious learners of today.

My Story
Establishing my Voice

I was a precocious child who created a very robust life for myself, experiencing everything as a new adventure. I adored Pippi Longstocking and would pretend scrub brushes were tied to my feet to wash the floors. Pippi was my childhood hero. She had an adventurous spirit that was inside of me; she had a confident persona that inspired everyone around her. She wanted others to follow her ideas. I was Pippi Longstocking and wanted to be important like she was and have others follow my ideas.

I have spent my life's work helping others feel important because that is what I wanted to feel and did not want to feel invisible. I wanted to matter and would always make sure people knew I was in the room. In my classrooms, I would be the first to raise my hand to answer a question the teacher asked or the first to raise my hand because I had a question for the teacher.

Always an enthusiastically inspired learner, I would go up to people and introduce myself to learn who they were. I have realized as an adult, I did this to find out who they were *and* so they would know who I was. I wanted to be noticed and now know that the concept I was feeling all those years is *Ubuntu*, meaning, I become myself from you.

An educator my whole life, my greatest desire has been to share my enthusiasm for learning. And it still is. As a ten year old, I had craft classes in my basement for the neighborhood kids because I wanted to share my joy of creating. Today, I enthusiastically share ideas to help struggling readers as well as my new healthy recipes for all who will listen.

When I was fifteen, I had a summer camp in my family's garage in our suburb. I spent all the money the neighbors paid me for their three- and four-year-old children on materials for the camp. By the end of summer, with a profit of $0, the camp was a success. The children enthusiastically attended every day. We had a purpose together, learning and sharing.

After five decades of sharing and teaching, I have a better sense of what works and what does not. Feeling able, feeling inspired works well; feeling shame, feeling less than does not work so well. In fact, these feelings of learners can be counterproductive; they often cause one to shut down.

There are experiences I had in childhood as a school student that inspired my ideas and passion as a professional educator. For example, in fourth grade, we were asked to write a paragraph about every president and vice president in the United States. I remember wondering why we had to copy out of the encyclopedia. I really did not learn anything. What I did love about the exercise in fourth grade was using my peacock-blue cartridge pen. The pen flowed so nicely, so comfortably across the lined notebook paper. I still use a cartridge pen today, one my father gave me, with peacock-blue ink.

I remember debates in Mr. Natzke's eighth-grade class at Joseph Warren School in Chicago. I debated against David Henry, the eye doctor's son. I debated the merits of contact lenses, which were rather new in those days. I won the debate and my parents let me get contact lenses as a result of that debate and the research I had conducted. It made schoolwork real.

I went to Bowen High School in Chicago. It was the first time ever I enjoyed science class. Mr. Kinsey's passion and energy about science inspired me. The subject was not of great interest to me because there were so many new words that had no connection to my life; it felt like learning a foreign language. Mr. Kinsey showed us and had us experience these foreign words. Science had always been so elusive, and Mr. Kinsey made those new words come alive for me. I learned much later how science vocabulary is so elusive to students. Embedding them in real-life experiences guides understanding.

When I was fourteen, Martin Luther King Jr. was assassinated. I was in the lunchroom of Bowen High School in Chicago when we heard the news. The black students got on the tables and were chanting. I had never seen anything like that before and was scared. All the students were all sent home and I ran as fast as I could. My father called me from his grocery store on 47th and Cottage Grove Avenue and told me to stay home and not leave the house. Our diverse, well-integrated close neighborhood community was never the same. For the first time in my life it was split in half: black and white.

Soon after that, there was a great exodus from the South Side of Chicago. The children became the victims of the midnight white flight. We all left to various suburbs, some of us never to see each other for forty-five years. In my recent reconnection with my South Side friends, we are all sharing that we never felt connected in our new schools and suburbs like we did on the South Side. We are holding on to each other for dear life once again, reminiscing, remembering, reliving memories, and reconnecting in new friendships from the strong bonds we formed in our youth.

We share we were victims of war, uprooted from our homes, our neighborhood, friends, school, and we now have words for the feelings we had back then. This is my history, my content of Dr. Martin Luther King Jr. and how he affected my life. I have learned more about Dr. Martin Luther King Jr. over the years. The most important content about him, for me, is how the end of his life affected mine so dramatically.

Leaving the South Side was a powerful catalyst for me. I was uprooted from my familiar, comfortable surroundings to a new place, with new people, not feeling welcome or comfortable, and experiencing the unbearable feeling of invisibility. It took years for me to create my own comfort again, well into my adulthood.

I do not remember reading many fiction books as a child, except for Pippi because she had the kind of life I wanted. I was a voracious reader of the blue biographies in the school library. Although they followed a predictable pattern, I loved learning about other people and their woes and joys. While reading about other people, I found pieces of myself. Just like the people around me, I find myself in them. Feeling empty inside forced me to look to others to see what I wanted. That became my theme. I sought out people for the life they had, or so I thought they had, that I wanted. Some things fit; many did not.

Moving from Bowen High School to Glenbrook South High School; it felt like going to college. The classes were much more difficult. Always a good student, I was able to keep up. I enjoyed French class and the creative writing class, and have kept those writing pieces for four decades.

One very challenging class was Mr. Lyon's sociology. He assigned a research paper on a topic of our choice every month. I remember attempting the very first paper and had no idea how to write a research paper. Assumed I missed learning the process during my freshman year at Bowen, I suffered through the process and eventually developed a process that worked well for me using note cards.

This was the same process I would later use to teach students as a school librarian, RTW (Read, Think, and Write). Having choice in my topics gave me ownership. I wrote about powerful women—Emma Goldman and Isadora Duncan. I still remember how Isadora died by getting strangled by her neck scarf blowing out of the car window and wrapping around the rear tire! Isadora's dancing inspired my dancing throughout my lifetime.

My love of sharing throughout my childhood and adolescence turned into an interest in teaching by obtaining a degree at the University of Iowa in Elementary Education with a concentration in early childhood. I remember the Language Arts methods professor, who told me I would not make a good teacher because I could not follow her lesson plan template. Having turned in something creative, it was a good thing I had resilience. I did not listen and, most importantly, did not believe her. This was an important lesson in taking back my power from a person in an authoritative position.

Figure 2 displays a paper I wrote at the University of Iowa that reviewed the book *The Me Nobody Knows* by Stephen M. Joseph in 1971. It was a compilation of stories from the ghetto in New York. Although I did not live in a ghetto, I felt invisible as these students did and wanted my Voice to be heard. I wanted to matter. I had a self-poverty as these children, destitute of visibility and spent the rest of my life attempting to eradicate this sense of destitution. I was envious that these students were having a Voice, even though their words were very painful. Establishing a Voice through conversation and writing became a powerful theme for me as an educator.

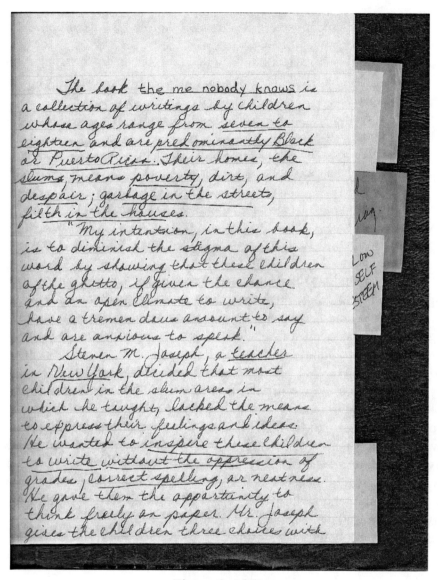

Figure 2, 1971

In the book, students were given three choices by Mr. Joseph:

1) Write about something that is important to them and sign their name. They can ask me to read it and discuss their writing.
2) Write something that is important to them and omit their name and turn it in.
3) Write something that is important to them and either sign their name or not, and not submit it.

What Mr. Joseph found was that with no stipulations or expectations on the students, the freedom of writing was more appealing to them than ever before. He also saw an honesty and Voice in his students, as they felt compelled to reveal and share.

While attending the University of Iowa, I had an inspiring opportunity to intern at Willowwind School, an educational alternative school in two houses right next to each other. The students were multi-age and learned interesting subjects such as calligraphy and Latin. It was a big caring family with relationship and learning as the primary focus.

Writers from the University of Iowa Writer's Workshop and other professors would send their children as an alternative to the public schools. Author John Irving's children were my students. Willowwind was a special place. There was a kitchen where breakfast was made every morning for the children. The children had to clean the house as well. They would sweep the floors and put all the things away that were used in school during the day. The rooms were so warm and lively with student learning. I loved Willowwind. It was a vibrant house of learning and relationships.

Willowwind students acting out the story *The Three Robbers*

I loved learning in college, and the most memorable class was linguistics. Learning the derivatives and patterns of words, how they were created, and all the forms they would take by themselves and in sentences intrigued me. One letter could change an entire meaning. My passion for vocabulary learning translates into my teaching today.

I also worked at the Iowa City Public Library with the reference librarians. One of the reference librarians was the community outreach librarian who sent me to work at the Iowa City County Jail to inspire the inmates to read books. It was there that I realized the power of conversation surrounding books. The inmates were more inspired to read when we would talk about what they read; having opportunity for relationship around text was powerful. I fell in love with books, words, phrases, sentences and paragraphs, and the conversation that surrounded all of these.

I was offered a teaching job at Willowwind but decided to attend graduate school in Library Science at the University of Oregon. My love of books and learning and my father's unexpected death in 1975 inspired me to go far away.

After obtaining my Masters of Library Science Degree at the University of Oregon, I was ready to come back home to the Chicago area. I began working as a school librarian; the entire library was content for the students. I loved that students had choice in what they wanted to read. Developing relationships and getting to know my students as readers and learners became my focus, so I could inspire them, find subjects and books they might be interested in.

In Oak Park where I was a school media specialist for fourteen years, I would keep piles on the back table of the library for individual students. One year, a parent donated a hundred dollars to the library for all the personal attention I had given her daughter in book recommendations. Her daughter and I had a special relationship through conversation about text and stories.

My favorite part about my position as a school librarian was storytelling. When I read stories, showed pictures, or read chapter books to older students, I was on stage, acting for them to feel a part of the book. One student said to me, "When you read to us, you are like my preacher." I smiled at his analogy and realized how my passion came out in storytelling.

When I was in Oak Park as the school librarian at Holmes School, I created RTW, Read/Think/Write. This emanated from my experience in fourth grade, when I copied out of the encyclopedia and my experience writing research papers monthly in Mr. Lyon's class. I did not want my students to copy out of books. I wanted to know what they were learning and how this new knowledge and information swirled around in their head as they processed.

I discovered something that was very interesting. It was not the lowest-ability students who would copy out of the books for their notes. They often were not able to understand everything they read. It was the higher-ability students who would copy; they did understand everything they read and wanted their words to sound just like the books.

The process of RTW taught students to read (R), put a bookmark in the place where they were reading, and close the book. Learners were to think (T) about what they read and what learning they derived most often, emanating from their conversing about their learning; then write (W) notes on note cards to remember their learning. No sentences, just notes—words and phrases. This would inhibit them from copying out of the books and, more importantly, value their learning by gaining confidence in composing their own words from their thoughts and feelings. Students would use RTW to do research projects from kindergarten through sixth grade every year. They would choose a subject of interest to them and study it for several weeks.

Students who experienced this research process became so adept and had such engaged interest that one year, we created sixth-grade debate teams against teams at the high school. My own debating experience in seventh grade at Joseph Warren School with Mr. Natzke inspired this opportunity for my students. The teachers, students, and I chose topics that held the interest of both groups, such as "should the drinking age be lowered?" It was a memorable experience as the teams worked together to debate against these older students. I suspect when the sixth grade students eventually went to Oak Park River Forest High School, they were a bit more comfortable as a result of that experience, as well as more prepared in their research abilities.

Early in my school library career, I became a mother. My children would have birthday parties with all of their classmates. Comfortable with handling an entire class, I would not allow my kids to invite some and not all. Creating a party of twenty-five was a wonderful celebration. Inclusion is in my fabric of being. I did not ever want anyone to feel excluded, a feeling that was unbearable to me.

My first year as principal in 1994, I devoted all my energy into creating our learning community—my teachers, students, parents, and myself. By the spring of my first year, our state reading scores were abysmal. My Assistant Superintendent of Curriculum met with me and questioned, "Remember what you said about test scores in your interview: 'If you had a strong curriculum the test scores would follow'? Does this mean you don't have a good, solid curriculum?" I walked out devastated.

Did it?

I went back to my teachers and said, "We have a problem. I know you are all teaching reading well, but our scores are not representing what is happening in your classrooms. We need to figure out how to solve this dilemma." And we did. We brought in a consultant to share the progression of reading skills. For one school year, we created and developed Leading to Reading (LTR), a basic skills curriculum for learning to read instruction. We implemented the following year in grades one through three, and a couple of years later, due to increased reading skill acquisition, we moved it to grades one and two. Thousands of students learned to read with LTR over the years at various schools. Many adults also learned the basic skills of reading with the LTR program.

As we moved forward with implementation, other schools learned about our success. In 2004, the Illinois IGAP (Illinois Goal Achievement Program) scores at Sipley School rose from #305 to #36 in the state among schools with double the per pupil expenditure. We were among the elite in state reading scores. With the success of LTR, I knew it could be useful to others so I shared at conferences. We had over 500 educators visit LTR over the thirteen-year period at Sipley School under my leadership.

Our students loved reading. As they learned to become proficient and confident readers, teachers created book collections in their classrooms to match. We provided book bags for each student to hold the collection of materials, books, and magazines they would be reading throughout the day. When I was a librarian, I had this vision of classrooms looking like libraries. I wanted students to have the choice of reading material and it finally happened. I had achieved my dream.

Another critical moment in my principalship was when my teachers and I had said, "Enough!" to the writing of our students. I had visited a classroom and stayed while the teacher stepped out. I sat in the rocking chair and the students brought their writing pieces and read me their writing to the prompt, "Why I want a dog, or cat, or whatever pet they wanted." My first thought was how cruel this was for the students who were living with eight or so people in a two-bedroom apartment. Worse yet was the writing. It all sounded the same, cloned writing. No personality, no Voice. I had attempted some professional development for my teachers in writing over the years. This time, as I exposed my lack of enthusiasm for reading our student writing in our school, the teachers began to admit they did not like to read it, teach it, or create space in their week for it.

Something had to change. Just as we had done with the reading, we took on this challenge together. The primary teachers and I investigated available curriculum programs to guide better writing, and as we began to prepare a launch of a whole new writing program, this time, the intermediate teachers said, "We're in. We are not waiting." After the opening year of adult writing workshops and our first few weeks with students, our Voices, teachers, and students emerged. One teacher shared her own journey.

Becoming a WRITER...

My journey toward writing....

Years ago Ellie came to school and told us to write. She gave reasons, shared pieces, and made it clear how important writing was. Well, I felt "what a waste of time, two hours of this??" I don't need to write I need to know how to teach writing. I listened, I tried to pay attention, I played the game, and I wrote... a list of chores that needed to be done. Few years later | Robyne did the same thing, I played the game again. And then Robyne did it again, this time I wrote about my goddaughter and it was god-awful writing. "Anyone want to share? HA!! And again, only this time she gave us fancy journals. Looking back at these sessions, I would have to compare myself to many students in classrooms. I was not available for writing and frustrated by what was being asked of me as students/audience members are not available for learning.

And why should I write??? Someone would get into my life, I

Another teacher emailed me on the weekend after the Friday adult workshop. She was a four-year young teacher.

11

Dear Robyne,
I want to thank you for our writing in-service on Friday. No one has ever asked me before, in school or otherwise, to write something that was important to me.

She had written academic papers, about things, about others, but nowhere in any of her classrooms or courses for twenty years had any of her teachers asked her to write something that mattered to her. I was thrilled she finally had the chance and we were offering this for our students.

Our students' writing improved immediately. Teachers guided students to write what was inside of them. I remember a sixth-grade teacher bringing me a wadded-up piece of paper she found in her garbage. She had seen her student toss it in the garbage can during writing. The student had written about how he didn't like how his mother cried all the time from the loss of his baby brother. He wrote he was sad too but did not want to cry in front of his mother. The teacher asked me, "Should I give this to the social worker?"

I advised her not to and suggested he was not ready. It was wonderful that we provided him the opportunity to begin his healing through writing, but he threw it away and was not ready to share. I assured her he would over time. And he did. Eventually, he wrote a poignant piece about the loss of his brother and the effect on various family members.

If I had to encapsulate the most critical learning in my 45 years as an educator, it would be the social and emotional capacities that create community and fosters the greatest achievements - academically and in life. Learning about self and others through conversation and connections deepens understanding of relational rapport that serves as the greatest gift of education.

This concept is best described as Ubuntu. *I am because we are.* And I add, *We are because I am.* Honoring self, feeling valued, feeling that one's contribution is welcomed and matters. I matter. You matter. I cannot do this alone. We are the links in the chain that hold the strong connections to our education. These two components, self and others create a learning community that abounds in achievement and success.

About Education
How do we end the learning starvation diet in our schools?

There are so many children in poverty of learning in our schools. They are not receiving a healthy education to inspire lifelong learning. They are being fed processed, unhealthy curriculum. They are getting on the scale too many times to test their efforts. We are actually creating nonreaders, nonwriters, and non-thinkers by replacing vibrant learning environments with test preparation and test completion.

Students' learning capacities do not grow by taking tests. These capacities develop by engaging students in a vigorous curriculum, where their brains are active in asking their own questions, not filling in the blanks of others. Students thrive on a healthy education plan, one with rich nutrients, rich vitamins, and delicious; they prosper on gourmet curriculum. We want healthy, vibrant, energetic learning for our children, where they thrive as learners.

Our starvation diet has actually caused the disease of disconnection, and a powerful example of this disconnection is in the story of Erin Gruwell's *Freedom Writers*. Her former students describe the inevitable paths they were headed—jail, early pregnancies, destined to drop out of high school. The connections she created in her classroom, relational and academic transformed these students who were certain their life outcome would be destitute. Erin Gruwell gave them a purpose. She educated them. She inspired them. She created a place in her classroom and school where her students felt they mattered in the world. She gave value to their Voice and, therefore, to who they were as human beings. She began by giving value to their content; then the world content had roots to grow.

Self-content is the foundation for learning other content. One of Erin Gruwell's students shares her epiphany while reading the story of Anne Frank, where she began to realize it was just like the gang warfare in her Long Beach neighborhood. Her living content gave roots to her learning about the world, and about history. Erin Gruwell ended learning poverty in her classroom.

We are obsessed with the "knowing" state, not the learning. We trick ourselves into thinking we are charting progress to see how much is actually learned. Yet, it is the charting that seems to matter. We do not have much space for discussing text material or even wondering what interests our students. We provide everything we believe students should learn. There has been little space for student interest in the school curriculum to develop, yet, humans have insatiable curiosity.

When we provide space for the "not knowing" and "discovering" state of learning, the knowing often unravels, adding new layers of knowledge and experience. I went into my dissertation research with a sense of knowing having been an administrator for almost twenty years, and when I listened to teachers outside of my school, my comfort zone, my knowing came apart. I took in these new Voices, mixed them with what I had known and lived in my own school and created a whole new learning for myself, one that had space for possibilities.

In our schools, we are spending too much time modeling for students to do what we instruct, students answering our questions, following scripted, robotic curricula and not enough on students' divergent opportunities and asking their own questions. I call this "Simon Says" teaching.

When we trust and honor the Stages of Learning (Appendix Two), we develop reverence for the learners' path and pace of learning. This is what our schools are for and what being educated means. It is to have reverence for the learning process. In my work with an adolescent learning to read, I discovered he labored on every word in the column of the first syllable pattern. We stopped after four words. I knew enough. I knew he did not have a sense of the pattern and was guessing based on the letters in the words. No further assessments were needed. Uncovering more detail about what Terry *could not do* would have brought his intense shame into our sessions. There was no place for that in this new learning zone.

My guidance emanated from watching him and listening to him as a learner. It is not in a teacher's manual. What I did was not written with instructions anywhere. I listened to him. I learned from him. I then knew how to guide and build on what he was learning. I made sure he felt successful in his learning in each session. We rarely discussed what was to come. We always celebrated what had been learned.

As I worked with Terry, I realized he was not only learning the basic skills of reading better to access in his brain, he was also accessing the joy of really learning these words, a new experience for him after guessing for so many years. He owned them because they were coming easily to him, for the first time. He laughed at the silly short vowel sentences he practiced reading in text. He read the paragraphs to himself, then aloud. I told him, "You astound us!" He asked, "What is that word?" I told him, "You amaze us, wow us, because you are such a confident reader now." He said, "I like that word. Can I use it in a sentence? 'Melody, can I astound you?'" Terry loves new words.

Terry's vocabulary instruction began to come from the words in our conversation that appealed to him. By honoring his learning process, Terry was 100 percent successful in our sessions every time. He would leave our sessions feeling full, satiated in his learning, not depleted and starving, or shamed.

How do we provide gourmet, healthy curriculum in our schools? We do it by providing all students that which keeps them engaged. We do it by honoring their self content. We do it by honoring our learners and their process of learning. We live in a world that is seeking more all the time. Our world is seeking bigger, better, faster, thinner, where the concept of *enough* is not really important. We cannot stand still at enough. We treat our students that way in school. We tell them that today is not enough. We tell them it is more important to constantly prepare for tomorrow. This never *enoughness* is creating poverty in our schools.

This constant attention on the future, this obsession with today not mattering as much as the test next week is creating an anxiety filled system that is not working for anyone. It is not working for teachers who feel they need to close their doors for real learning to occur. They close their doors for fear the principal will pass by and overhear an

15

organic conversation about something that has happened in their neighborhood. How shameful that student conversations about their lives is "off topic."

We live in a fast forward world. Our Halloween aisles sprout in early September. And by mid-October, almost two weeks before the actual holiday, the aisles become barren, making way for November and December holidays. Easter eggs sprout on our shelves at the midnight hour following Valentine's Day. School special education meetings are about next year, in high school...what about now? What is needed today?

I sat in a special education meeting for a seventh-grade student, in March, who did not want to go to school. The principal talked about "when Nalia goes to high school." I said, hopefully in a kind way, "Mr. Principal, I hope we will not have to worry about that. For now, and the purpose of this meeting, we need to concentrate on what we can do so she wants to come to school *tomorrow*."

There is a great divide between learning in schools and that which we need to cover for the test. We have tests that will measure exact answers, smartness, and levels. Do these tests really measure student-learning growth and capacities? What do these tests do for us? We give these tests so much power. And it is replacing precious learning time and devastating our education system. We have the most extensive comprehensive tests ever in our history and a billion dollar literacy curriculum publishing market, and we still have a significant national percentage of nonreaders.

About Schools

How can we develop the capacities for students to thrive in our schools?

Imagine if we created space and places where learning is the priority, processes are valued more than final outcomes, and adventurous and purposeful wandering are the norm. Today, there are so few opportunities where our students have choice in their content learning.

Teachers have so much they want students to learn, so they attempt to fill them every day with new information and instructions. Yet, we know as adults, our greatest learning stems from our intrinsic desire to learn, not from the filling from others. It happens best when we fill ourselves. And it starts with knowing our own content, our *self-content*, and asking our own questions.

The first half of my career, I was a school librarian/media specialist, learning center director. The name morphed as the technology expanded. I developed RTW, which was Read/Think/Write, so students would not copy out of the books they were using for research. They would read something, think about what they read, write about their new knowledge. RTW was a feature of the research process for students to do and learn with a myriad of resources in the library. Students would choose a topic of interest, develop their own questions to inspire their research, find materials and learn anything they wanted to about their topics.

The teachers and I taught how to ask the questions to navigate their learning. It was a wonderful, divergent way to inspire students to create learning for themselves. Students developed and controlled the questions and sought answers in text and other places they would find. This emanated from my experience in fourth grade, when we copied out of the encyclopedia, which felt so empty.

Jamie McKenzie calls this *purposeful wandering*, learning to question to wonder to learn. I remember one student who studied trains in fifth grade and wanted to study trains again in sixth grade. His sixth-grade teacher wanted him to pick a new topic. I encouraged her to let him search more about trains. He was a year older now. and had much more to learn. I later learned this student became an engineer as an adult, with a concentration on our rail systems. I suspect the research he did in fifth and sixth grade had great value as the seeds were planted for his greatest interest and chosen career.

The research skills of my students were so strong that by sixth grade, they debated against teams at Oak Park River Forest High School. My students' research skills were highly developed; they had better skills than the high school students.

When we provide ways for our students to identify their own content and create content, they learn about themselves. We want them to bring their learning to others in the classroom. We want other students to learn about them. For example, if we are studying important people in history, we can first ask. "Who are the important people in their lives?" We can ask our students to find out who in their lives lived when Martin Luther King Jr. was assassinated. What were these people doing, and how did it affect their lives? How about 9/11, where were they or someone they knew? How did it affect their lives? One of my childhood friends shared the story of her memory when Dr. Martin Luther King Jr. was killed. This was her "self-content" at age fourteen, yet she had never shared it in forty-five years, in school or otherwise.

I, too, have thought of that day for decades. History impacts us more when we have perspective. This is my memory. My father had a tailor shop on 64th and Halsted. He was called the "blue-eyed soul brother" because he helped so many underprivileged black kids in the ghetto. He bailed quite a few boys in the hood out of trouble and made them promise to go to night school and make something out of their lives. That day of MLK's assassination. a Black Stone Ranger came into his store, told him to go home. get his kids from school, and not come back for a few weeks. He told my dad to put a sign that read "Black is Beautiful" in his store window and that he would make sure nothing happened to it. Every store in his neighborhood was burned down except for his. My dad is still alive but very sick, and that memory of my father is responsible for every good thing I have done in my life. He will forever be my hero and my role model. Martin Luther King Jr. was a man "who had a dream," and sometimes, dreams can become realities.

—Vicki Lehrner Adams

There are so many ways we can inspire students to engage in our content. And we must provide the fertile ground for them to know their content first, then, we can inspire them to learn about content that is important to us. Honoring students' content empowers them in their learning. By empowering our students to make decisions about their learning, value their self-content and that of each other's self-content, we develop their integrity and success as learners in a caring learning community.

How can we maximize the learning in our schools? What would this look like? What would a school environment look like where students thrive academically, socially, and emotionally, caring for each others' learning as much as their own?

This is my dream.

At *Ubuntu* School each student matters and deserves to be honored as a capable, dynamic, and successful learner. Every student matters. Students are empowered as the masters of their learning. When educators believe that each child can and will learn and listen to their students as to the best way, learners thrive. There is no need to create a ceiling for anyone. Sometimes educators have to believe in students until they believe in themselves. It is the educators' responsibility to create an environment by providing opportunities for learners to grow together. Learners have their own content; they have their own stories. When we listen to these seed stories, outside content connects, meshes, and flourishes in the learner. Sharing creates caring and synergy for our learners to be inspired, engaged, and successful.

Here is what happens at *Ubuntu* School: I am because we are.

Learners arrive in the morning with teachers welcoming them to school with a big smile, saying, "I am so happy you are here today." Children also greet each other, every single person; not just their friends, but each person as they enter. All learners (including adults) feel welcomed and happy to be there. Each student has a chance to meet with a Caring Coach (adult or another student) who has been carefully paired to listen and care about the student to begin their day. Caring Coaches help with any concerns a learner has about his work or day, or anything, so his learning availability is optimized. After the Caring Connection opportunity, students go to their areas for learning.

Liz Murray in *Breaking Night* attributes her academic success (happening in high school for the first time in her life) to the relationships she had with her teachers, "My feelings about the teachers *were* my feelings about the school." When Liz had teachers at previous schools, they treated her as a victim of her family circumstances, being raised by drug addicts. When she had the teachers at Prep School in New York City who believed in her as a capable learner, she rose to their high standard. The teachers at *Ubuntu* School will be like those at Prep School in New York City.

In each classroom, there are tables with side drawers to hold students' personal materials for learning. On the tables are collective materials for learning; pens, pencils, sticky notes, clips, anything they need throughout their day. Learners share. The classroom looks more like the art room than a traditional classroom. Then learners gather in a circle to welcome the day together in a morning meeting. The teacher has a connection opportunity for students to deepen their relationships to start their day. Today they are taking time to share about a person who is very important to them in their life.

Learners return to their group tables and have an opportunity to write some things about that important person and why she or he is so important. Then they share their thoughts and feelings with a neighbor, then at their table. Each takes about fifteen to twenty minutes to write this person a letter to compose from the heart how important he or she is to them. After some time with the writing workshop process, learners build the capacity to work through their own writing dilemmas. Feeling angst, stuck, drawing or thinking for a time without writing is all part of the process. Teachers too often solve the struggles for students robbing of them of the opportunity to know how to solve for themselves.

If I would write to an important person in my life, I write to my mother about her joyfulness. She brings sunshine into every room with her grand smile and enthusiastic spirit. I write:

Dear Mom,

You mean the world to me. You have such joy in your day and it spills out to everyone around you. You love to be with people and you love adventure. When someone suggests an outing, I don't think I have ever heard you say, "I don't think I want to." We always hear, "Yes, that sounds fun." You are happy in advance. It is a beautiful way to approach life. You matter so much to me. You have been such an inspiration of joy and enthusiasm. You are a ray of sunshine in every room you enter and everywhere you go. Your friends adore you. Your smile and bright spirit are endearing and contagious.

After the learners write, the teacher may gather everyone for a mini-lesson (about 10 minutes) s/he has discerned from their previous writing sessions that most of the students would benefit. It could be substantive like creating a metaphor in writing, or it could be grammatical, such as using commas.

Writing is expressive production. Students learn best and will use grammar best when they need to use it. Only the most basic of instruction on the up front in the earliest learning of writing gives time and space for students to develop their Voice. If there is too much instruction in writing, the conventions take up the space, at the neglect of Voice. Other skills unfold in mini lessons, gradually accumulating as needed in writing. Voice matters most and when given the most attention and time, becomes strong and confident. Conventions and structures begin to frame the Voice.

Capital letters begin sentences.

Periods or exclamations end them.

Commas are in the middle.

That is it!

When students begin to use quotations, they love to learn the punctuation that surrounds them.

Writing is a time of expression. All the reading and receiving of information the learners have now engaged in releases in their expressiveness. They become their writing and their writing becomes them. They use their words to share who they are, share their new learning, share their feelings, whatever they want to express. The writing environment is established.

There is a conferring table. Writers choose pens or computer or switch back and forth. The learners get into the zone of writing, the merging of their mind and heart. However, *their* ideas always matter first.

Early in the year, learners have established themselves as writers and list topics they are inspired to express in writing. This is an ongoing list to be referred to as often as needed. Learners choose the genres of writing they feel compelled to use. The teacher and students are continuously sharing text to model various writing genres as they build and strengthen connections with each other in their community of learners.

Writers write for an hour at least. It is essential they learn this stamina to get into their writing zone. It is quite all right they end a session in the middle of a piece of writing. It is actually preferred because then, when they start up again, they can gain quick momentum since they already have the work going. Often, starting is harder than keeping going. Most often, when the hour is up, students will say, "I feel like we just started." This is evidence of experiencing the *writing zone*.

Writers confer with each other and with the teacher. Sometimes, two-people conferences work well because one student can benefit from the other's writing dilemmas. Learners often feel alone in their challenges and gain power in their learning when knowing others have challenges. Sometimes, students don't know what they need in their writing and questions from one student can help another. For example, the teacher says, "When you write about your grandfather, I don't know much about him. Can you tell me some things about him?" Questioning empowers students to make decisions about the substance of their writing.

When writing time ends, learners may choose a word, phrase, sentence, or paragraph they particularly want to share. There are five shares per session. Every person gets a chance to share in a week. Students learn to discern which is the most important for them in their sharing. They carefully choose those words that have most meaning to them.

After the learners share their writing, they move about in physical exercise of some sort to recharge and shift to receptive learning and processing, the time for reading. Writing comes first because it honors self-content. The day starts out with what is important to them in their lives and their learning. It empowers learners to think about themselves and share with others and creates connections.

Writing is expressive, an opportunity to compose words, phrases, sentences, paragraphs, chapters. It is a way to merge what is in their hearts and minds, and be produced on paper. Writing and expressing well establishes the learner's Voice. When writing begins the morning, composers are provided the opportunity to clear space for new learning.

Reading is receptive. It is where we take in someone else's words and ideas. We learn and we often feel when we read the words of someone else. We take in this information and we choose what becomes part of us. We are compelled to respond to what we read—we can write in a journal, mark pages with sticky notes, have conversation with others, and we want to act on our new intake.

If we own the books, we can write in the books. I write in all my books and have my own conversation with the author. I treat books like a blog. I argue and scream at them, thank them for their words, and cry with them, because they have so poignantly articulated *my* thoughts and feelings. When we perceive material we read as alive text, hearing the writers' voices in our head, we interact more dynamically.

In Ubuntu classrooms, learners have a collection of textual materials for their choice at their tables. They choose one piece of text they can spend the time it takes to get into the zone. There is a vibrant feel in the room—an energy of learning and sharing. Students interact with the text they are reading, with sticky notes, writing in a journal, and in conversation with each other. During silent time reading, students who feel compelled to share at that moment can write their responses in a thought bubble to share when conversation occurs.

This reading time will take over an hour. Students' needs dictate how the teacher spends time and organizes students in small groups for learning. The teacher may sit with a carefully designed small group or one-on-one conversation about a student's reading. There may be a small group choosing syllable patterns they need to practice. Learning to read and reading to learn create the substance throughout reading time. Words are honored. It is through the reading and expressing of words in conversation that enhances the capacities of rich literacy.

When reading time comes to a close, the teacher warns learners with about fifteen to twenty minutes to finish. Now learners can meet in small groups to share about their reading and learning for about fifteen minutes or more with each other. Dynamic conversations ensue from this lively learning time. Connections occur as each learner's sharing is valued with each other.

A whole group lesson might occur next. The teacher has chosen a book to read aloud and shares a comprehension strategy that is useful while reading. The teacher reads the classic tale, *Caps for Sale,* and shares how inferences are often required while reading. The teacher provides an example of text that states explicit information such as, "On every branch sat a monkey. On every monkey was a gray, or a brown, or a blue, or a red cap!" The teacher also shares text that requires an informed inference, such as. 'You monkeys, you,' he said, shaking a finger at them, 'you give me back my caps.' But the monkeys only shook their fingers back at them and said. 'Tsz, tsz, tsz.'" Students learn that the monkeys are copying every move of the peddler even though it is never stated directly in the book. Students vigorously seek and share inferences they find in their own reading materials.

The read aloud also provides for creating common vocabulary and background knowledge for the class. In the book illustrated above, students learn the word peddler and explore renderings of the country. Conversation around theme and story also become common knowledge among the students which creates relational connections throughout the year. Often, learners will relate their independent books with the class read aloud. "Remember when we read…"

It is now time for a lengthier span of physical activity. Outside, fresh air is always preferable. However, inside exercises and stretches are also useful and helpful for students to keep their learning adrenalin going.

This is the entire morning. Students are inspired learners immersed in literacy opportunities. The morning has filled the students. They have engaged in self-content. Their Voice has been valued. They have had choice in their learning. They have read and had conversation about their reading. They are now ready to listen and learn other new things the teacher has chosen.

Self-content is what is inside of ourselves—our knowledge, thoughts and feelings, and our stories and memories. Self-content is our perception of memories with others. We own this. No one else does. When we give time and space to students' self-content, we honor them as human beings and provide opportunities for them to feel that they matter to us and their classmates.

Why is reading and writing all morning? Literacy is the foundation of all learning. Reading, listening, viewing are intakes of information; writing, composing, talking are expressive. A strong foundation of literacy development provides capacities for all content learning—math, science, social studies, fine arts, physical health and wellness, and all derivatives. All of these subjects are included in the morning literacy work as well as further developed in the afternoon.

There are symbols and vocabulary to understand in all subject areas. There is basic vocabulary and more enriching vocabulary devoted to the study of the content. There is analytical thinking in the content. There are comprehension capacities that help us establish understanding of content. (Appendix Three: Capacities of Literacy Comprehension.)

When literacy is developed solidly in the morning, it then continues throughout the day in all other content areas. Literacy evangelist Ellin Keene shares a poignant story of her experience in her book, *To Understand*, Chapter 2, Seeking Understanding in Our minds, in Our Lives. (Heinemann, 2008)

I remember going home with great enthusiasm and telling my husband, David, "These kids were unbelievable in their book clubs today. They were able to probe a single idea to extraordinary depth. It's like they were holding a diamond up to the light to examine its facets—only the diamond was an idea. They could have talked for hours. I am so blow away by these kids. They can really surprise you, you know? I'm so lucky to be a teacher—these are the moments, I tell you. They are so smart. This is why I teach!" I could really get on a roll.

He looked at me with more than a little skepticism—eye rolling, even. I think he expected me to burst into the first verse of *God Bless America*. My idealism at a fever pitch, I took myself a bit too seriously. I intoned something about how I touched the future and shook my head with feigned sadness for him, saying, "You poor thing—consigned to practice law for the rest of your life." He listened to this dramatic drivel for months before asking dryly, 'Why don't they do that *every day.*'

What was happening in this classroom?

Learners were:

1) Thinking, wondering, and searching ...*like they were holding a diamond up to examine its facets- only the diamond was an idea.* (Students were probing to extraordinary depth)
2) Examining ideas and all facets (looking closely from many angles)
3) Thoroughly engaged in the literacy process. *They could have talked for hours.* (engaging in the learning/literacy process, text and talk)
4) Developing self efficacy as a learner. *They are so smart.*

Efficacy is how one perceives themselves and their capacities for success. When one's self efficacy is healthy and strong, learning confidence is developed, motivating further experiences. Self efficacy can enhance with others providing feedback, however, others come and go. We have our own perceptions every minute. It is vital to continually nurture our own self efficacy. A person with a strong self efficacy seeks and becomes energized with new learning experiences, while someone with a tentative self efficacy prefers sameness.

These are noble goals in education. These two paragraphs describe the literacy capacities we want to develop in our learners. Although Keene uses fiction as an example, all reading content may be applied to these descriptions. Each morning of *Ubuntu* School is a daily opportunity for students to experience the vibrant learning together Ellin Keene describes.

The afternoon is devoted to more specific subjects, such as math, science, social studies, and fine arts: music, art, drama, and dance. Textual material, reading, and writing are also involved in these subjects. Writing offers learners a venue to make sense of the text and new learning with which they interact.

A teacher in *Ubuntu* School values learners' questions as much as they value their own. They value the students' content and stories *more* than they value their curriculum materials. Ubuntu teachers value the historical figures in their students' lives *more* than they value notable figures in textbooks. Their students know the teacher wants to hear their stories. Students know they matter to their teacher. And, as importantly, they know their content and stories matter to their classmates. And their classmates' content and stories matter to them. This creates a bond of collective strength and learning that make all learners feel smart. Each person rises to his or her highest level of achievement by helping and receiving help alike. This is *Ubuntu*. Our own personal best is because of our work with others. *I am because we are.*

In schools today, we often create an environment where students are required to do more listening than interacting. Listening is the least effective mode for our learning to have enduring value.

In our *Ubuntu* School, students are filled with interactive, constructive learning. They create content and they learn content. Students experience, interact with content, and process in a variety of ways to keep learning alive. They learn that what *they* learn and what *they* have to say matters. They know their contributions are valuable.

They have choice in their learning. They share what is important to them. Relationships are crucial to their learning in school.

When students have choice in content, they feel connected to school. They feel it is real. When the teachers do all the choosing, the students do not feel ownership, often feel disconnected. Students become vessels for the teacher's control and choice. This is Paolo Freire's banking model; teachers deposit into the student's depositories (*Pedagogy of the Oppressed*, 1970). It is empty, non-enduring learning most of the time.

When students are allowed to engage in constructivist learning rather than just being receptacles for information, they have a stake in their learning in a way that fills them. Students can be given a choice in a theme. For example, learning about past and present artists provides anchors for time periods that informs of critical moments in our history. There are many artists for students to study. It is not essential that teachers choose all who will be studied. Providing time for students to search and choose artists empowers them in taking charge of their own learning.

John Dewey, in *The Child and the Curriculum*: "The child is the starting point, the centre, and the end. His development, his growth, is the ideal. It alone furnishes the standard. To the growth of the child all studies are subservient...It is he and not the subject matter which determines both quality and quantity of learning." (*The Middle Works*, 1899-1924, p. 276)

At *Ubuntu* School, learners are engaged in their own research projects throughout the year. They are the captains of their learning, seeking, and following their own wonderings. Learners become inspired and insatiable from the choice of topic to all the twists and turns of navigation. They are entrenched in their learning and, as a result, become empowered masters of the learning process.

Social and emotional learning is threaded throughout the day with intentional opportunities such as class meetings to promote collective problem solving. Cross-age experiences develop caring, understanding, and empathy for various age levels. For example, each 5th grade student in a classroom paired with a 2nd grade student provides an opportunity to build a significant relationship that affects other cross age relationships.

When two students research about an animal in the school library together, they form a bond socially and in academic collaboration. This bond creates an honoring of each other's contribution to the relationship. This bond will extend to the peers of the others.

In my school, one younger student passed a note to his sixth grade buddy in the hall. It read, "I hope you did good on your test I know you tried your best" The sixth grade student enthusiastically shared it with his peers and teacher. The caring exemplified from this one youngster spread throughout the entire classroom.

At Sipley School we implemented *Caring School Community* ^{TM}, created at Developmental Studies Center which includes detailed information for teachers to provide effective social/ emotional opportunities in class meeting formats, cross age buddies, schoolwide events, and homeside activities The ultimate is developing strong relational rapport which includes learning about self, about others, and about self with others = community.

Another intentional offering to develop social and emotional capacities is Caring Connections. This is a method where students are paired with an adult, and eventually other students, called Caring Coaches, for connections throughout their day to help them navigate more problematic behaviors. Caring Coach sessions are effective for any student to have their Voice exclusively heard by an adult who cares.

When students with emotional and behavioral challenges are paired with Caring Coaches, this may be a critical significant relationship with an adult who becomes their advocate in school.

In these Caring Coach sessions, the coach guides students in self discovery to articulate the messages of their behaviors which minimizes or eliminates their need to act out. These sessions offer students opportunities to feel safe to use words instead of behaviors to express their Voice.

All learners, including teachers, increase their capacities emotionally for themselves and socially with each other. All content opportunities honor individuality, promote connectivity, compassion, and empathy. Our experience with *Caring School Community* ^{TM}

expanded our hearts at Sipley School as academic learning cultivated our minds.

In *Ubuntu* School, class meetings occur routinely, giving children the guidance and opportunity to figure out the dilemmas they encounter. When children are empowered to solve their problems together, they see things adults do not always see, and they become vested in the solution. When I was a principal, fourth-grade students invited me into their classroom meeting to help solve a problem in the lunchroom. They were concerned that the first-grade students took so long to load their trays with lunch items that the fourth-grade students did not have enough time to eat their lunch.

By allowing students to offer solutions to their dilemma, powerful things happen. First, they become creative and have conversation that sparks ideas in each other. Where community caring is the norm, their ideas are empathic rather than blaming.

The solution of this class illustrates a wonderful example of compassion. This class decided to pair up one fourth-grade student with a first-grade student. In buddy fashion, each fourth grade student would help the first-grade students load their trays quicker and all would get the same amount of time to eat their lunch. This solution not only solved the problem, the fourth-grade students filled themselves with caring and compassion in helpful roles rather than blaming roles of the slowness of the first-grade students.

In fourteen years, the staff and I had not solved this dilemma. When the students were given the opportunity to solve, they created a thoughtful, caring solution for everyone! The residual effects of increased relationships were bountiful!

On the closing day of the week at *Ubuntu* School, there is a learning celebration with opportunities for readers and writers to share their learning. What content and process has each learner contributed and received in our learning community? What have they learned about their learning this week (understanding their own metacognitive processes)? How did they see themselves as learners and about how they worked with others? What did they learn about each other as learners? What works best for them? What did they learn from others and what did they learn about others? What questions did they have at the start of the week? What were they still wondering about?

This closing opportunity is a message to them their learning and learning processes are important as a unique individual and in the learning community. What they choose to share is also valued. Learners become adept at describing their own learning and progress. Their listening to one another enriches their learning as a community. A learner begins with, "I learned that..." which sparks in another learner, then another, with flowing content of individual and group learning.

It is vital for learners to be able to articulate their learning because it makes it concrete for them. As they educate others, their learning becomes solidified, having enduring value. Their ability to articulate gives them ownership. Their learning is not for the teacher, or for a test. It is for right now and the continuous purpose of more learning, and to perceive oneself as a scholar. Their learning is enough, for today.

What students learn they can articulate, and what they can articulate, they have learned. It is not more important if it is on a test and less important if it is not. This is a strong message. Their learning is ENOUGH. Their learning is what matters most. Revering themselves as successful learners is their greatest achievement and a motivator for more.

When we feel we do not measure up to another's standards, or worse, measure up to our own as created by others, we are left feeling empty, less than, and this impedes the learning process, slows us down, and worse, erodes our self efficacy as a learner. When we have students share with a neighbor, we are affirming their learning to each other, honoring the valuable contribution of each learner. The more we do this, the more we are affirming their learning and building their self efficacy as a learner and as a community of learners.

Ranking learners in the classroom is unhealthy and quite detrimental to the learning of the group and to individuals. A hierarchical system of ranking smartness has damaged our entire society. When we feel enough, we feel fulfilled, which speeds the process. Enoughness gives us energy. It feeds us to keep going; even when the going gets rough, we still keep going because once we know enoughness and we want more of that feeling. We want to stay in that state because it fills us.

I just described the school and classroom I wanted to be in, I wanted for my own children, and I want for yours. I created the environment that offers an honoring community, where all learners feel valuable in their contributions in the classroom. They are all writers; they are all readers. They are all learners. They are each successful. What they know and learn matters and what they write matters most.

This is my dream. From my knowledge and experience in education for almost six decades, I predict *Ubuntu* School would provide a different outcome than we get in our schools right now. We would have more inspired and less controlled learners. Our students would do the wondering. Our teachers would no longer be anxious, nor will our children. We would have a new kind of vibrant energy, one that celebrates learning in a new way. We would have an energy that celebrates and promotes more questions than answers.

Students would feel safe and scholarly because they are successful in their learning every day. Students would create connections accumulating in lasting relationships. Students would be discovering, experiencing, and constructing their learning, creating, wondering, caring, and sharing every day. In *Ubuntu* School, students value each other's contributions in their work together, developing a collective pride towards their common purpose of learning and solving life dilemmas.

Ubuntu School will honor ENOUGH.

We are at times too ready to believe that the present is the only possible state of things.

—Marcel Proust (1871-1922) —

Learning Substance (Curriculum)
How do we create more learning for students?

Education is about learning of a lasting nature, how to do things (like decoding unknown words), acquiring knowledge (learning from others and text), creating meaning, developing the powers of reason and judgment (as one develops self-content), and portraying that learning when interested.

Teachers most often make the judgments about the learning and always have the power. We give students an abundance of things we have decided they should learn and then test for "mastery" of that learning. Mastery is typically the same for all. Who decides what should be mastered and what does not, the curriculum publishers, the teachers? What about the learners? What if learners decide for themselves what they will master?

Published curriculums provide instructions for teachers and students, content to be learned, activities to do, and questions for teachers to ask. It is like a meal in a box. The means to the end is a test. These published curriculums usually lack opportunities for creating a community of learners in the classroom. Sharing in a classroom is crucial to building the self efficacy of learners.

Learners need to know their learning is not only important for themselves; they also contribute to the learning of the community. It is not healthy to the group to view the learning as a hierarchy, with some better than others, or some smarter than others or someone's knowledge and experience more important than someone else's. When we allow students to contribute content to the classroom, we give them power in their learning. We give a strong message that which has meaning in their lives, what has meaning to them as people, also has meaning to our classroom community.

However, the published curriculum programs often create superficial learning that passes through our brains without creating connections to remain. Authentic learning emanates from merging self-content with new content. This learning creates enduring value, that which can be accessed at a later point in time.

The published programs often offer empty curriculum, like empty calories. There is rarely time for deep discussion about the things we feel while we are reading. We have to move on. For the sake of time and volume, we stay at the surface level of learning. There is too much to cover. If we truly learn, there is enduring value. Much of what we do in school does not have enduring value. It is akin to processed foods—processed curriculum that has the illusion of filling, but little to no nutritional or healthy value and, eventually, damaging.

We want healthy, fulfilling curriculum, creating opportunities for growth, understanding of text and how that text matters in our lives, and how that text means something to what we experience on a daily basis or something from our past. For example, what do we learn from the book, *A Star of Hope*? What do we know about what happened during the Holocaust? And why is that important to us in the present time, in our daily lives?

Why do we learn about important people in history? What do they represent about our past and how our lives unfold? Why these historical figures, and not others? Erin Gruwell's students became entrenched in learning history by having opportunities to examine their own lives first, so the new knowledge had something to attach and mesh. What about the important people in our families? Why are they important? What we learn about ourselves and our families is crucial to content engagement. Often, the ability to connect self-content is relegated to enrichment activities, if there is time. Enrichment opportunities often offer the most robust engagement in the textbooks.

Currently, teaching is all about modeling, cramming, stuffing, tracking, monitoring, and preparing for the tests. Ellin Keene describes the teacher as playing tennis- hitting the balls to the students fast and furious. My university students regularly talked of the robotic curriculum they were forced to use. What if we created space for undirected learning in our schools? What if we empowered our learners with making decisions to navigate their own learning?

At *Ubuntu* School, I envision curriculum like a menu. There are appetizers—those small items that are important for our education, where smaller is better, to whet the appetite. Learners choose their entrees and side items for greater depth and understanding. Sharing of entrees family style is a way of creating a collaborative learning environment.

Students' energy sparks learning together. And our ultimate goal is a healthy gourmet curriculum. We provide an opportunity for our students to create content, create their own data they are inspired to conduct and examine. When we allow students to help create curriculum, they become invested in their learning. Their content is vital to our world.

We allow buzz words in education that create loyal bandwagons. Often the intention is good, yet can eventually become toxic in the following. The pervasive idea of "rigorous" is one such toxic buzz word. This word creates a very tight, confining image. Rigorous feels strict, adherence, harsh, discipline, hardship, and inflexibility. We want rigor for our students? I think rather we want vigor. Vigorous is healthy, active, lively, vitality, energetic, powerful, vibrant learning.

One of my Teach for America students created a unit of study where her Chicago inner city high school students could examine the data of drug dealers' earnings, a subject of great interest to them. The students became immersed in studying the research conducted at the University of Chicago. These high school students were scholars and came to the conclusion that drug dealers did not make the income they had envisioned. The "profession" was not as attractive to them from their findings. This authentic, engaging research sparked the students in academic research and answered their own circuitous questions like no other experience before, dispelling a myth they had idolized.

We want celebratory classrooms, where students are smiling, joyful, and divergent in their learning. Rigorous appears stifling, reductionistic, and convergent. Rigorous implies stringent rules, sameness, and robotic. Rigorous classrooms are not happy ones, and often create anxiety. Vigorous learning creates joy, inspiration, fulfilling learning.

Our gourmet school would have a vibrant feel, one where everyone wants to attend because it tastes so good, is so healthy, and provides the cheer, joy, and abundant learning for everyone. There is a vigorous energy of insatiable learning, often one thing leading to another with sharing at the core. I want to be in this school. So do you. We all want to be in this school because it feels so good and healthy to be a learner in this school. And the learners include the teachers. We are fulfilled and our learning grows rapidly.

The content for our students are guided by the Literacy Comprehension Capacities (Appendix Three). Students engage in noticing deeply, experiencing, wondering, making connections, developing relationships, finding patterns, honoring each others' contributions, creating meaning, engaging in action, reflection, and self-assessment of their work. We want our learners to honor their individual progress as they develop and increase their learning capacities over time.

There are basic skills to be acquired, such as decoding symbols in reading and math, encoding and producing symbols, such as letters and numbers, to create meaning. There are literacy capacities to be acquired, to know and understand and to be able to create meaning in all content areas. For example, a basic skill to be socially literate is the ability to welcome someone new when he or she enters your familiar space for the first time. The context can be a classroom, organization, group meeting, anyplace. This skill displays evidence of understanding another's emotion of fear upon entering an unfamiliar setting with new people (decoding), and displaying caring towards that person (encoding) with, "Welcome, so glad you are here." The behavior of welcoming also demonstrates the social capacity of reaching out and honoring others to help make them feel comfortable in new situations.

We want to provide enough experience in the basic skills so students feel successful in their learning and not feel shamed in their not learning. There is no grand standard for this learning and no one way that ensures all learners acquire the skills simultaneously. There will be outliers, those who learn more quickly and those who take more time. When we honor all rates of learning, Vygotsky's "zone of proximal development" is understood for our learners of basic skills. When learning in the zone, students sustain motivation when the going gets rough.

When students feel successful in learning to read words, phrases, sentences, paragraphs, pages, and chapters, they learn to appreciate text, what other people say, others' stories. When students feel cared about in their learning process, they are able to care for others, creating *Ubuntu*.

My work with Terry in his learning to read thoroughly convinced me how a learner becomes damaged in his or her learning process over time. He had developed such ineffective habits in his reading that it was painful for him. He was frustrated and angry and became highly skilled at avoiding and manipulating around his non-reading. A careful, delicate process was needed to build his self efficacy as a learner. He had been in a quicksand of failure, not knowing how to get out.

Every year Terry sank deeper and deeper, developing self-protection behaviors to create the illusion that he could read or the defense it did not matter to him. Terry's head was held high as he walked around the school hallways with four-inch wide textbooks he could not read. He needed to learn the basic skills in an orderly fashion, with success every step of the way. His "zone of proximal development" needed to be honored and sustained.

Reading, being receptive of content, comes first for learners as does taking in the world for a baby. Babies are looking and "reading" the world's symbols long before they are able to talk and express themselves through words. Children learn to identify letters before they can write them. As students' reading skills abilities expand, they also fall in love with creating their own text and telling their own stories. They learn they have a Voice that is important to themselves and to others.

With students and their self-content honored in *Ubuntu* School, writing becomes their ability to express what is inside themselves with words and sentences. They have a Voice inside that is exactly and uniquely theirs. They are not ranked where one person is valued more than another. Students who do not develop this sense of self worth and self efficacy as a learner soon fade in school and disengage or become robots, only able to do what is instructed and modeled.

When students continually synthesize their new learning with their existing knowledge and experience, they create new meaning for themselves and share with others. We want their learning to be vibrant. We also want our students to cultivate strong relationships with people, words, text, authors, various genres, ideas, and people. By reading and listening, they take in the world of what others say and then decide the importance. We want learners to read about children their age, people of their own culture, and other cultures.

We want our students to build their learning capacities as their own curiosity motivates them to be insatiable readers and sharers. We also want our learners to be drawn into a fantasy so unbelievable it creates awe and wonderment. We want our students to love language in the text and visuals to create their own through meaning, through discussion and writing. We want students to learn how to make decisions about words they use, how to create their own sentences that flow, and how to portray their authentic learning in writing not for the teacher, for themselves.

Can we write our own family history, one that we can pass on from generation to generation in our families? Let's be real about text material. Students do not read the 1,000-page textbooks we put in front of them. There are few people who actually read them, probably teachers. Students do not. How do we get our historical information if it is not from the textbook? In real time, when we get inspired by a topic or we have a question, then we search for information. We become informed about topics that peak our interest.

I was such an inspired learner as a child, insatiable with my own questions, only not in the classroom. In the classroom, my learning was for the teacher, not myself. I longed to be in a critical learning classroom where students could ask the questions (as I was in my head all the time). I craved to create meaning as well as learn topics of others. I had so many conversations of learning in my head that had no place in school. Organic conversations are not usually part of system curriculum.

In *Ubuntu* School, topics learned are organic, not just teacher selected. In a critical learning classroom, each learner has the opportunity to create learning and meaning for themselves. The learning is cultivated among the interests and needs of the learners in the room, and the questions in the learners' brains that spark like fireworks. There is no planning of elaborate lessons or schemes to get students to learn.

The students and teacher create the learning environment together. Learners thrive in their garnering from text and expressing their thoughts and feelings in their own words. Learners make authentic connections from the content in their lives and feel educated as they accumulate and make sense of the content of the world.

In my sessions with Terry, he was always asking questions about things he was wondering about. "How old is Muhammad Ali? Does he have Alzheimer's? One question led to another. He was an inspired learner. "What is that word?" And he wrote the new words down, learning authentic vocabulary because they were emanating from questions he was asking, vocabulary that had enduring value. His vocabulary increased exponentially through his reading and wondering.

Another toxic buzz word associated with curriculum these days is "fidelity." Fidelity means to follow a curriculum program exactly as the authors intended. It means to implement only what is written in the manual—do not add anything, enrich, or be creative. It means to not go off on any tangents that might be relevant or not relevant. Adhere to the instructions of the published program.

Fidelity is not about the learners; it is about control. And it is about the ability to track data for the program. Does this program work? If not followed with fidelity, then one cannot say whether it works or not. Curriculum cannot be controlled in a petri dish as science can. Our schools have human beings. One cannot predict the questions learners will ask. Great teachers listen to these questions. These questions may navigate from the intended fidelity of the program.

Great teachers care about what students think and feel and wonder about. Great teachers customize learning to each student for success at the cost of fidelity, which is about adherence to the program, *not* the student. The systems are put in place for all but do not work for all; sometimes not even for most. The more we customize for the learners we know well, the greater achievement each student experiences. Our fidelity *must* be to the students.

The use of *Strive* was customized for Terry. There is no teacher's manual or set of instructions. The only fidelity was to Terry learning the basic syllable patterns that forms most words so he would read with facile and not guess which was ineffective. Terry made the decisions for his learning. He set the pace, determined which words he felt he knew well and which words he would practice. Terry learned how much he needed to practice for his learning to solidify.

Terry also discovered very personalized learning such as mixing up the letters of b, d, and sometimes p. He also discovered that he was reading the beginning of words and not always the endings, and how one letter can change the meaning of words. In his reading about Archie Manning, the word son is very different from sons. Soon after identifying this, Terry changed the habit and paid particular attention to the endings of words while he read.

During my last year as principal, I was attending my thirty-seventh year of curriculum reviews. In the process, the committee listened to publisher's presentations about their programs. I remember thinking I was sitting in a sales pitch for a Florida condo. They all started out the same: "Our program is research based." I heard, "Everybody says so." Then, "This has all the features you could possibly want—literacy connections, videos, student engagement, essential concepts and skills, activities for ESL." I heard, "Wonderful amenities, swimming pool, steam shower, on the ocean." Are they really all they say they are? They say they assure our students will score high on tests.

Curriculum marketers use all the latest buzz terms—rigorous, standards based, achievement based, test prep embedded. Does this mean our students will have great science learning experiences or they will be able to pass a test? We have allowed assessment to replace curriculum. It is like saying the number on the scale is the sole measure of our overall health.

In a speech given at National Louis University at the Reading Leadership Institute on January 2012, Dr. Peter Johnston answered the question, "If children are expected to become the next leaders of our nation, then why do adults expect them to remain pliant and obedient?" with the following:

- A singular focus on academics doesn't serve kids, teachers, or society well;
- Teachers need to take seriously the fact that the adult is not the only teacher in the room;
- Kids' social imagination should be taken more seriously;
- Focusing on children's engagement changes everything; and
- Making meaning is good; doing meaningful things are better.

My experiences with comprehensive published programs, the food buffet varieties that offer gluttonous arrays of options, are they provide very little that teachers find effective in classrooms. The free materials that often come with these expensive programs are titillating, yet useless. When we developed a new reading curriculum in my school district, the teachers chose a quality anthology of text material in grades three through five.

The salesman of the anthology was attempting to provide all the *free* things if we would buy Package A. Looking for a discount without all of the free materials, I told him, "Frankly, the free materials are not of high quality and the teachers who perused them did not find anything worthwhile to use in their classrooms." His response was, "I don't know about that, I am just a salesman." This spoke volumes to me about what was happening to curricula in our schools. The billion-dollar industry in educational publishing was about marketing, not necessarily quality.

It is time we offer healthy, quality, substantive curriculum experiences for our learners; that which has enduring learning value in their lives. These curriculum opportunities would develop our Literacy Comprehension Capacities (Appendix Three) as well as honor the relationships enhanced throughout the process.

Terry became a successful reader in ten weeks, at age thirteen, for the first time in his life. He had been to reputable schools with excellent resources and education specialists. How was he learning now and why had it not happened before? The very first day I met with

Terry, I asked his permission to help him. He had a small sparkle in his eye with a cautious grin, one small pinhole of hope, that this time, maybe it would work for him. He read the first four words, laboriously, pronouncing sounds, and with no sense of syllable pattern recognition.

I stopped right there and had all the assessment needed. I knew where to begin. Terry could not read. Had I continued with more assessments, he would have felt increasing shame. It was not necessary and a damaging way to begin our relationship. He was a successful learner quickly, and continued in that mode with very gradual accumulation of achievement, one syllable pattern and one word in that pattern at a time.

After Terry guessed at the first four words, I said to him, "We can stop right here. I hear you guessing at the words based on the letters in the word." This is why you are struggling with all of your words. I will teach you the patterns and you will be able to read easily." I explained the first syllable pattern (letter, vowel, letter), had him explain it to me and practice some words, and in a moment, his reading improved. He reread the first four words, this time, with ease. He then chose the words he felt he needed to continue to practice until our next session.

From that first day, Terry began to believe in himself in a new way. He was reading intentionally, now accessing syllable patterns that were more effective than guessing. His feeling of "I can't" shifted to "I can." Every session since that first day, every exchange we had affirmed his new belief: "I can." In ten weeks, Terry had learned more than half the syllable patterns in words and increased two grade levels in reading. I had created energy for him to believe he was a successful learner, until he believed in himself, which came rather quickly.

Each student needs to believe in themselves as a learner, honor their own individual pace, best learning modes, and know their contribution is valued. Our assessments force our learners to walk the hall of shame again and again and again. This systemic cruelty to children is abusive and unconscionable and it happens every day to our children in most schools!

Emotions and Behaviors

How do we develop social and emotional literacy in our schools?

Emotions are the glue of learning and living. Emotional intelligence can be traced back to the 1900s and popularized for schools when Howard Gardner informed us of multiple intelligences in the early '80s. Daniel Goleman continued framing the importance of our (emotional quotient) E.Q. in the 90s.

Yet we still, as a society, define smart as one dimensional. Every Teach for America student in my university courses is in awe of what they learn from their special education students. They became humbled in their ranked intelligence by the intelligence that surrounds them. Why do we continue to stay so one dimensional? Why is our definition of smartness so narrow? We all experience it is not true.

We think we can separate students' emotions from their learning and it is not possible. Learning and remembering is emotive. Emotions are often the glue that allows us to infuse the new content we learn with our self content. If we want students to remember things, we have to allow emotions and feelings to be honored. Students need to feel safe in the classroom, and that includes their emotions as well.

If we suppress human emotions, students' authentic learning is compromised. When students' emotions become intensified from something in school or out, they are often not available for the learning experiences. If we allow the emotions, students' learning is comprehensive and their learning has a greater chance of enduring.

Educators separate emotions from learning in their classrooms and schools because they separate it for themselves. We are holistic human beings. It is not possible to separate and feel whole. Brene' Brown calls this wholehearted living. School has become almost exclusively about academics rather than humanity, and that is not serving us well anymore.

The international organization CASEL (Collaborative for Academic, Social and Emotional Learning) has promoted legislation for requiring Social and Emotional Learning standards across the nation, and uses the main argument that promoting SEL enhances academic achievement.

I propose that social and emotional growth are not only fundamental in and of themselves, but are the most important development skills our schools can provide for our learners, and academics are second. Social emotional literacy enhances our self efficacy as human beings, which provides us emotional and social capacities necessary in all human endeavors.

We do not do much in schools to help students know how to develop healthy relationships. We often do the opposite. Healthier social and emotional capacities are needed everywhere, in our homes, our schools, and our organizations of work—*everywhere*. With this lack of relationship-developing skills in our society, we typically react to the social and emotional needs rather than understand their meanings as important messages.

In addition, we usually respond to crises, when the circumstances rise to an egregious level. When educators have many of these crises, they are motivated to look for programs such as "bullying." The problem is not about the bully; it is about what has happened in the school culture that someone feels s/he needs to employ bullying behavior. How can we care for those who take advantage of others and help them feel more a part of the culture no longer necessitating the alienating behavior?

Social emotional programs are for everyone, not just relegated to those who seem outcast. Social emotional programs offer intentional opportunities for everyone to grow in their understanding of self and in their relationships with others. If a student is compliant, does that mean s/he is socially and emotionally healthy in school? If a student does not appear to have any needs, does that mean s/he does not have any?

Often, educators believe our schools can only function well with overt compliance, like squaring our corners in the hallways. I believe compliance is highly overrated. Students want to be understood and treated like individuals. Students who do not comply speak to us through their behaviors. Behaviors are loud messages to us and often inform us that something is not quite right. If we pay close attention to those messages, and not concentrate on punishing the behaviors, we can create a different trajectory for that student over time.

Demerits, detentions, and punishments do not work at changing behaviors for chronic students because the punishments are extrinsic. They are done to us. They do not change behaviors. The only time behaviors change is when we are ready to change them; we become intrinsically motivated and careful guidance creates success.

Natural consequences ensue. But we have a system of demerits that do not work. If students do not do their homework, demerits are given. They do not care about the punishment. Doing homework is not a priority for them. They see no need.

I remember early in my career the principal observed me as a school librarian, reading a story to a first-grade class. In the post observation conference, he said to me, "You let Damon crawl on the floor and did not discipline him."

I said, "Yes, I did that on purpose; all the other students were listening and viewing the wonderful illustrations in this compelling story. If I had called attention to him, it would have distracted the entire class. By NOT calling attention to him, Damon was the only one distracted. He needed to crawl and squirm on the floor." I had no evidence that he was not listening to the story.

He replied, "I never thought of that."

This was my early lesson that many educators and administrators pay more attention to compliance and the system than to an individual.

We are obsessed with compliance. We demand it with symbols such as uniforms, and with rules such as walking along straight lines in the hallways, marks on bathroom walls indicating where to pull the paper towels, distributing demerits and detentions for doing what is not the norm, or NOT doing what is the norm. Yet, are some of these things really important? We say it is for their own good, or when they go elsewhere and have to follow their rules. We all learn that things operate differently in different places, our homes, even with each classroom. In one classroom, the teacher is okay with casual language. In another, it is not okay.

In one school I know of, the morning announcements on the intercom end with, "Make a great academic day." Just the sound of it concerns me. This infers to all the students to split off from their whole selves—it intimates that what is in a textbook is more important than who they are.

We have so many students in our nation who speak loudly to us through their behaviors. We often perceive this as, "I don't care about school," "I don't want to do this," or "Why do I have to do this anyway?" These are not questions or statements about learning. They are about the emotional state of the learner. We are all inherently hardwired to be learners. We crave learning. It is as much our sustenance as food. For those who struggle in our schools, shame and defeat becomes their norm. The system labels them as failures and they believe it. Their behavior becomes their armor or protection. It takes passionate and patient educators to help these struggling students to change their belief of themselves.

Relationships/Creating *Ubuntu*
How do we create *WE* as our highest virtue?

Relationships are the heart of all our work in school and out. Relationship building is crucial in the school setting and any organization. The greater the depth of relationships in our schools, the greater likelihood achievement increases. Building relationships among students, as well as teacher and students, creates the connections needed for students to thrive in their education.

Often, teachers build their relationship with each student, yet do not nurture the relationships among the students with each other. This is crucial to developing a caring community, one where students have compassion for each other as humans and as learners. Imagine a community where students help each other in the learning process and care about each other's learning as much as their own.

Social emotional literacy is an integral part of building these relationships. It is developing a relationship with oneself that is filling and complete. It is building connections in pairs, small groups, and as a whole group community. It takes intentional work to do this. When teachers provide opportunities for students to create connections that develop social and emotional capacities, students feel included and honored by each other.

In a classroom, we have daily opportunities for students to make connections and build relationships that create *Ubuntu*. In an Ubuntu classroom, students work hard for each other and for themselves. All learners feel valued as an integral part of the learning environment. Each member feels they matter and feels enough. No one feels less than or not enough.

Educators have highly revered Benjamin Bloom's taxonomy of cognitive domain of learning since 1956, which begins with basic, often rote learning to the highest levels of metacognitive processing. Bloom created an affective taxonomy that was equally important, yet separated and actually ignored over the years.

This affective domain speaks to crucial capacities in social and emotional learning necessary for individuals' well-being as well as working together in organizations, i.e., schools, workplaces, communities, and other organizations. These affective skills include learning awareness of feelings and emotions in self and others, valuing others for their contributions, honoring diversity, and the ability to work together cohesively as a caring and compassionate group.

When educators seek bully programs, they envision a program that would change the bully, their attitudes and behaviors, so others would not be affected. The irony is that the program needed is not about the bully at all. It is about creating a culture in the classroom and the whole school that develops the concept of *Ubuntu*, inclusivity. It is about creating a culture that offers intentional practice in the affective domain of humanity, one that honors each member's contributions, feelings, and experiences so students do not feel isolated and become bullies. The "bucket filling" concept is powerful for young students to understand how to include people, show caring for others, and in so doing, feeling good about oneself.

During my final years as a principal our intentional work to develop social emotional learning capacities began with the Caring School Community (CSC)^{TM} program developed by Developmental Studies Center. Our teachers' back-to-school professional development was two days, filled with CSC opportunities to experience what it would feel like in our classrooms. It was transformational. Children, staff, and parents all felt the changes happening in our school.

When the children began school, I went to each classroom and read the book, *Have you Filled a Bucket Today?* (McCloud, 2006) I also read the book to parents at our Back-to-School night. Bucket filling became our goal behavior. Bucket filling was demonstrated all over the school. Staff and students would enthusiastically share the caring behaviors to the teachers, to me, at meetings; caring and compassion spread throughout the school like a contagion.

During the winter break, I was sitting in my office, with only the custodial crew in the building. The quiet technology provider asked to speak to me. He sat down across from my desk and shared, "I don't know what is happening here this year, but your school is not like the others I visit. Your students are so kind and caring. Usually, I am unnoticed as I lay out my tools and work on things. Here, when I begin to clean up my tools, your students ask me if I need help and begin gathering my tools to put in my container. Your students are so helpful."

We did have scuffles now and then. When two students were brought into my office after an argument, the first thing I did was to have them read the bucket book, each student alternating reading a page. When they were finished, I would say, "Please think about why you were brought here and how you might have been a bucket filler instead."

Each child would describe a new behavior they could have employed to replace their old one. In 100 percent of the cases, each child would apologize to the other, a humbled, genuine apology. I did not ask them to do this. It emanated from their reviewing the bucket-filling concept and intrinsically recognizing they did not demonstrate a caring behavior.

I would then ask them if they would like to be a bucket filler for the rest of the day, and they would leave my office proudly displaying the joyous sprouted bucket logo sticker on their shirt. The students' understanding of their own emotional and social behaviors transformed before. A punishment was not effective in creating these new behaviors.

Caring School Community^{TM} teaches students to problem solve their dilemmas collaboratively. I was invited to a fourth-grade problem solving class meeting where the students were complaining about the lunch hostess who did not smile and appeared sometimes mean to the students. One student then suggested, "Why don't we smile at her and ask her how her day is going?" I got the chills as this nine-year young child suggested changing her own behavior to elicit a new behavior from the adult. I was filled as an educator that Tamara suggested the "bucket-filling" way.

When I returned to the class to see how things were going in the lunchroom, the students had wonderful stories of joy, and the new smiles they created for the lunch hostess, all emanating from them.

They had experienced the power of change in someone else by changing themselves. They were bucket fillers.

At the university, most of my students in the "Teach for America" program are serving as special education teachers; they teach the most challenging students in our schools. We call them special education students because they present challenges in their learning over the years and display similar characteristics. Special education students are often viewed by the regular education teachers as "those students," implying they are not "their students."

The classroom teachers often do not know what or how to teach the special education students. These students pose a challenge for their teachers in the same way learning is a challenge for themselves. And often, their teachers do not know what works best for them. They often try system after system and method after method.

Special education students are so often lackluster in their learning, lacking confidence, and revere themselves as non-learners, or worse, as failures, because the system continually tells them so. These children begin each lesson with "I can't" or "I don't know," which impedes learning unnecessarily. When they learn things, they very often surprise themselves. They have spent so much time, especially by high school, engaging in struggled learning that revering themselves as a learner is foreign to them. They most often revere themselves as non-learners, incapable. In regards to school, their inner voice bellows, "I can't."

A musician shared with me her "dyslexia" experience as a child. She storied, "I was put in the *dumb* group with three other students. We were made fun of and even looked down upon by the teacher. I felt so ashamed as a child." She then continued to tell me she is a voracious reader as an adult today after teaching herself how to read. She has remained close with two of the other students in her class as a child, bonding in their memory of shame together. They are all accomplished musicians as adults. I am embarrassed for the system that shamed these impressionable young learners as they began their life in school.

I have such reverence for the TFA teachers in my courses. They commit two years of their life to teach in some of the most difficult circumstances imaginable. In this very hard time, they are extremely passionate about what they do. They put their hearts and souls into their students and schools. As my university students have told me horrific stories about their schools, I would respond, "I marvel that your students even come to school." They have failed as learners by the definition the system has determined. They revere themselves as non-learners in most circumstances. And the students in high school have been doing this for years!

I have told my university students, "Your students come because of the connections they feel and the hope that just once, and let it be you, they will get educated, feel connected to you as a teacher, and school will be a successful place for them."

On a daily basis, my university students do not think they are doing enough. They see what their students need and feel they are not meeting all of those needs. This is overwhelming to them. I attempt to help reframe their thinking to believe they are doing enough, and more than enough in the most important aspect. They care. They put most of their energies into developing strong relationships with their students. This is enough. This will sustain their students for a very long time, maybe *forever*.

I tell my university students, "Through all the bravado these students have to demonstrate they do not want to learn, they are learning. They are successful in keeping you there with them, teaching them no matter how hard they try to make you leave, you stay. And this is what matters most. You are not giving up on these students because they have so often given up on themselves long ago." It is the relationship around learning that is creating the most value for these students.

In *Breaking Night*, Liz Murray speaks about her curriculum: "I knew that what I adored about school was that each of my assignments—readings, essays, or in-class presentations—was inseparable from my relationships with my teachers and with my new friends at Prep...I loved it for what it provided me access to: bonds with people I grew to cherish." (Murray, 2012, p. 265)

In my literacy classes at the university, teachers create customized learning plans for their students. First, they need to learn about the students they choose, and determine what would work best. For a final project, they choose one student to focus their creation of a literacy learning plan. They choose a student who they are drawn to.

When I have asked my students why they chose their particular learners, I received answers such as "I am him when I was young." And "S/he struggles like I did." These are crucial views we have of our students. We often see ourselves in our students because they are us. They are people who have stories of joy and struggles. Which ones are most like us, and as importantly, which ones are not?

I would tell my students, "Although you relate in many ways, your students are not you in some ways; they do not have the same backgrounds, experiences, travels, family structures." Many of my TFA students have travelled outside of the United States. It is crucial that you get to know who they are, what matters to them, so you can learn about them, learn about their self-content. Then you can teach them. They need to let you in. They need to let you have a relationship with them. And when you do, they soar."

And they do.

One of my greatest teacher influences is Erin Gruwell of *Freedom Writers*. She so beautifully portrays how important it is for all of us to tell our stories. When we tell our stories, we matter. We are enough. Our Voice breathes our life through words. Our Voice breathes our stories through words. We own our stories; they are uniquely ours. We have many stories, many experiences and relationships as seen through our eyes. We own our lives, every single moment. Even if someone ignores or dismisses them, we still own them. We have the right and privilege to keep our stories inside of us however we like. We can share them as opportunities or we can let them hold us hostage. Revealing our stories can be healing and help create connections deepening relationships.

Liz Murray in *Breaking Night* had not felt successful as a learner in any school environment until high school, when honoring relationships were formed, first and foremost. She had to know her teachers cared about her as a person before she could learn from them. Our starvation diet in education has actually caused the disease of disconnection, and our jails are filled with evidence of this disconnection.

Listening to Erin Gruwell's former students, the relational rapport through the connections she created in her classroom transformed students who thought their life outcome would be jail. She gave them a purpose; she inspired and educated them, made them feel they mattered in school and in the world. She gave value to their Voice, and therefore to each one of them as human beings. Most importantly, Erin Gruwell created community and developed *Ubuntu*.

Each student's success was a direct result of the work they did and the relationships they formed, together. They revered their individual success as the success of their community. And their peers' success mattered to them as much as their own achievement.

Data

How do we create and use data to serve us well?

What is data? Data is information, evidence, and ways of understanding. It is collected in and for a variety of reasons. We want to be informed, we seek patterns; we use data to assist in our decision making. We are a society titillated by numeric data. Higher numbers usually means greater evidence, more, and better.

By focusing on (quantitative) numeric data, we neglect a whole body of evidence that provides extensive, often more meaningful information that helps us guide our decision making. For example, how do we know a student is progressing in their learning?

When I observed in classrooms as a principal, body language of the students identified their engagement, their facial expressions, their ability to articulate to me what they were doing. I observed what students would do if they appeared confused. Would they ask a friend or the teacher? Observing the careful nuances in classrooms informed me about student learning behaviors more than any test was able to convey. Conversations with a teacher often portray more extensive evidence of a child's reading than the system's tests reveal.

When we collect and analyze data, we are like detectives, looking for clues and patterns. When a child reads with us, we have opportunities for observations of many ways they approach their reading.

Do they read with even flow?

Do they stop frequently?

Are they deliberate and slow? Is this evidence of decoding ability or deep thinking while reading?

My own understanding of data transformed during my doctoral studies. My dissertation research revealed data about teachers that could not be captured on any survey, or bubble sheets. My initial questions attempted to gather quantitative data regarding implementation and change.

How many students?

How many teachers?

What were the scores?

What were the trends before and after?

As my insatiable curiosity evolved, my questions morphed into qualitative wondering.

Why and why not?

How?

What were your experiences?

I realized even though my early questions were framed to collect quantity, they would actually elicit narrow answers, albeit easy to sort and classify.

In the very first interview, my first question provided such depth and understanding of what happens with change in a school, I abandoned all other questions. The teacher conveyed her experience personally, her experience working with others, her emotions, her beliefs. Her body language spoke to me; so did her silence. Each sentence was packed with data uncovering layers of understanding that quantitative data could not possibly reveal.

In that interview, I gave up control- which my early questions attempted- seeking answers that fit my questions. I watched my data unfold in data stories that provided rich and compelling evidence of change in schools.

Our obsession with data has driven learning out of our schools. We are a society that believes others have the answer. We call it data. We crave data. We love the buzz "research based." We want to know what others feel and think because we so often don't trust our own judgments. When others support what we think, we then feel justified. When they don't, we feel shamed for thinking otherwise. What we think and feel are not enough. So we seek data. We seek answers from the data. However, everything is getting research based these days. Something works for someone or many someones, and that becomes research. Most tend to think that wide data (quantitative) is more valuable than deep data.

Deep data is qualitative and gets to the heart of the matter. Deep data involves uncovering secrets that do not get divulged in wide data. Wide data has a reductionistic manner. Wide data does not get to the layers where emotion lies or at the feelings that are uncovered over time. Wide data gets at the surface levels, many surface levels.

How much is enough data? Are 10,000, 1,000, or 100 pieces of data enough? What about a dozen? What if it is only one? Is the testimony of one person enough? What if it is the testimony of a famous person? What if the data comes from inside of you? What if data shows one student has learned to read for the first time at age 13; does that count? Some of my collected data emanates from having 10,000 conversations with educators over a forty-year period. Does this count as enough data?

My data for this book comes from several sources that go very deep. When data goes deep, it uncovers the whys more thoroughly. I am my first subject, first and foremost from my own experiences in school, as a learner myself and among other learners. I first knew about education from my own school experiences as a child. For example, when I had to copy out of the encyclopedia in fourth grade, I wanted my learning to be important, not my copying.

My life became the inspiration for the life I created for others. My school experiences catapulted the school experiences I designed for others. Not feeling part of a community in school, I was very social outside of school. I remember school as being this cold, unfeeling environment; we squared our corners in the hallways, military style. No talking, no conversation, no learning together. My head exploded with questions all day long from my desire to learn. The teachers were not very interested in *my* questions.

Because I wanted to learn things of significance to me, I created environments for my students to generate learning that was of significance to them. Students are inspired, passionate learners. School can nurture or squelch this desire. In today's world of obsessive modeling (Simon Says teaching, do as I do), students are choosing their learning outside of school more and more, where they have some control over their learning and resources to satiate their desires and wondering.

I then learned about students through my own children, David and Greg, as well as the students who were in my schools. What I learned is that students want to feel important to the teacher and to each other.

They want to feel welcomed and included in the classroom community, just like they do outside of the school.

My data from my own two children is a small sample, but a significant one because I had a very close, personal look at each child and his school experience. David was an engaged learner. He wanted to please the teacher and do everything right. He doubted his own efforts and ability as he continuously measured himself against those who appeared more capable. He was acutely aware of others who seemed to do things more easily than he did.

David did not allow himself the opportunity to enjoy the Starter and Practice Learning stage (Appendix Two). This worked against him for most of his schooling and bothered him in the classrooms that operated in a hierarchy, where smartness was ranked and appeared privileged. Classrooms where students were all valued for their contributions worked better for David. He always raised his hand, to be noticed and also because he had questions. He was an inspired learner, always wanting to know more. David was not confident in his own abilities. At three years of age on the ice rink for his very first skating lesson, he was all clad head to toe in a bulky red snowsuit. I had not paid much attention to the fact that he was so bundled for protection he had absolutely no sense of balance.

The Ridgeland Ice Rink in Oak Park was divided into graduated abilities, the most advanced at the farthest end. I watched my son from the bleachers as he stood still on the oval-shaped ice rink, looking at the far end of the ice. I knew, as his eyes glared to the right, he was not looking at the next level, but the most advanced level way at the end of the rink. And I knew he was thinking to himself, *How do I get from here to there?* He was not paying attention at all to the varying levels of advancement it took to get there. He did not notice the stages in between, the stages of approximation and practice we need to go through to get to the more advanced place.

This is how David's life played has out. We still joke about the red snowsuit syndrome—worrying about the most advanced stage of learning when there are several stages to pass through. When David was getting his Master's Degree in Educational Leadership, he said to me, "How will I ever know enough to be an administrator?" I replied,

"Just like you learned to skate, one foot at a time; one moment, one day at a time." In fifth grade, his teacher, Sue McConnell, recognized this and brilliantly put him in the highest spelling group, although he was an average to just below in spelling. She knew this would boost his self-esteem and he would rise to the challenge. And it worked!

Greg, my younger son, has a very different story. Greg wanted to be invisible in the classroom. I would meet with his teacher at the parent/teacher conference in November and would provide relief for the teacher: "You probably don't know Greg very well; he prefers it that way. He usually has a pact with his teachers when school starts each year. He won't ask you any questions and he doesn't want you to ask him any."

Greg did not want to be noticed. He was very compliant. The teacher smiled and shared what a nice boy Greg was, always well behaved, and quiet. I had known that about his learning style. The teacher did not usually offer any more than that. She did not know him much as a person or as a learner. That always saddened me. I wanted the teachers to know my child. He was so special to me.

There were a few teachers over the years who knew Greg. The first one was in sixth grade; the teacher was new to the school, as was Greg, and they bonded in their newness. The next teacher was in junior high, who knew Greg struggled in reading. She did not know exactly what his struggle was, but she knew he was not a confident reader. The third was a social studies teacher who taught the required eighth grade U.S. constitution test with drama. Greg learned what he needed to and passed the test. The kinesthetic learning suited him well.

School content was never very important to Greg. However, he loved to learn and would watch the *National Geographic* channel daily. He still does. Greg has always been interested in many subjects. He loves science, animals, history. He just wasn't interested in what was taught in school.

I was always grateful that, at the very least, a few teachers knew my children well and guided them in building their self efficacy as a successful learner.

More Data

How can we expand our understanding of data?

If we view data as more than numbers, we expand our ways of knowing and understanding. My data emanates from my own students in classrooms over many years. As a teacher of preschool through eighth grades, I had a sense of knowing multiple ages interacting with content in the classroom and library where learning was allowed to be self-selected. There were no prescribed materials for me to use with students in our library.

I experienced energetic, vibrant learning with students, books, and endless possibilities for learning. I overheard one fourth-grade student commenting to his peer in line as the class left my library, "I think I learn more here than in the classroom." Students controlled their learning in my library and felt empowered.

More data emanates from observing teachers in classrooms. As a school administrator, I observed over a thousand lessons over the years. I watched closely what teachers and students did in the classroom. Observations revealed when learning worked well and what did not work so well. When students were thoroughly engaged, what was happening for that to be the case? I also noticed when students were disengaged, sometimes the teacher not knowing, and what was happening for that student to experience disengagement.

Studying human behavior in schools for forty years has revealed how behavior manifests in healthy and unhealthy ways and every way in between. These observations of human behavior as well as conversations serve as my data.

I studied the following questions seeking answers:

1. What is the teacher doing when students are engaged in the classroom?
2. What are the students doing when they are engaged in the classroom?

3. What is each child doing while the teacher is teaching, and what are the messages of the behaviors?

The answers vary in some situations; however, there are some generalizations that can be surmised:

1. When the teacher is paying more attention to the students than the content, the students are often more engaged.
2. When students are inspired to ask their own questions, their engagement is sustained.
3. When students are encouraged to contribute their own content, self-content (about their lives), they engage better to the content of others (the curriculum).
4. When students are allowed to interact with the content and each other, they are more engaged.
5. When teachers are honoring students by asking them questions so they can make decisions about their learning, this gives them authority in their learning, empowers them and builds their self efficacy as a learner.
6. When teachers ask divergent questions such as "Why do you think that?" rather than soliciting a predetermined answer, more hands go up and greater body language of thinking occurs.
7. The students in an engaged classroom honor each other and each member's contributions. They are engaging with text, creating meaning, and each other. They appear eager to be learning and doing what they are doing.
8. By noticing each child and not just the mass, students can appear compliant and not engaged.
9. Students can appear disengaged, fidgeting, or walking around the room and be totally engaged.
10. Listening to students and observing them provides a great deal about their learning needs and progress; more so than the assessments we conduct.

As my data expanded all these years, so did my knowledge, experience, and expertise in noticing what works well for learners in schools, and noticing what does not. I watched closely for inspired learners, demonstrated by students in their excitement in the library and in the classroom. Students asked their own questions and looked for answers, not always finding them, or finding them and wondering about the answers.

One student researched a topic for six weeks in the library, searching for answers to about thirty questions. When she was finished, she said, "Questions are so annoying. Even when you find answers, you always have more." Students conducted research in my library, navigated their own learning, chose topics, asked questions, were inspired and experienced the concept of "flow" (Csíkszentmihályi, 1990).

It saddened me over the years that this type of learning was enrichment, or supplementary, rather than the heart of the curriculum. In fact, reliance on standardized tests and answering preformed questions are the only measures valued in today's standardized world. We don't have measurements for student questioning, searching for their questions, and creating a wondering persona.

What if we offered in schools what we know as adults about learning and changing habits? We know they are personal choices, how and when, and we need to feel success by our own measures, not as measured against others. We learn, change habits, and sustain new ones best when intrinsically motivated, not when others force us to do the changing.

My life nearing six decades, and my data have inspired my ideas and passion about education, schools, classrooms, and learners and what environments create well-educated members of our society. Significant data can come from one learner. My work with Terry in his learning to read revealed on day one the shame he carried. When our session ended, he peeked out into the hallway, not wanting to leave until there were no students out there.

In our reading sessions, I discovered so many things about learning, shame, assessments, and success. In seven weeks, Terry became a confident reader for the first time in his life. How had the system eluded him all these years? He attended schools with good reputations. This success happened *without* assessments. It happened by creating the space for learning exactly what was needed to be learned for confident reading ability.

What would happen if we significantly reduced the data we collect? We have put so much emphasis on data and it is robbing of us the precious time our students could be learning. I believe with my whole being that we have had ENOUGH. We have had ENOUGH of the grand testing schemes, enough of giving our power of learning to others, stripping us of the dignity to be learners, to be in the stages of understanding (Appendix Two).

We have had ENOUGH of shaming students and continually telling them they are not enough. We have had ENOUGH of monitoring students to tears, to such a state of anxiety that it is a wonder they come to school at all. We have had ENOUGH of doing the same thing to teachers. If we create schools where learning is authentic, vibrant, exciting, and healthy, it would not take long to feel the prosperity of learning.

If we offer schools where students want to go every morning to learn because so do their teachers, they will be energized to continue their learning, ask questions, seek answers, create meaning, develop their learning capacities so their wondering about themselves and their world expands, rather than contracts.

We have had ENOUGH of what is not working. We want learning itself to be ENOUGH! Every single day we want enough to be the process rather than the outcomes that constrict what true education is about. We want our learners to feel what they do is enough and not feel what is ahead of them is so overwhelming they shut down, or become so competitive they are fraught with intense anxiety and compelled to stomp on everyone around them.

We have enough evidence that what we are doing is NOT working. We have had ENOUGH of the testing that wastes our precious learning time worrying, preparing, and obsessing about tests. What we have now is crucifying education. We have had ENOUGH!

Measurement

How can we measure differently so we feel rewarded, not punished?

Assessments are causing the *walk of shame*. Testing is our enemy. Instead of helping us and informing us, they punish us. It is like getting on the scale to weigh ourselves frequently throughout the day. The numbers do not tell us if we are healthy, if our food intake is of healthy nutritional value, or if we feel good that day. In fact, the number usually is counterproductive. The scale punishes us; it keeps us in a place of not being successful enough just as testing punishes our children and teachers.

I heard a story of an eight-year-old third-grade student who was pulling her eyebrows out because of the anxiety she felt towards the upcoming tests at school. I told her mother she could tell the teacher her daughter would not take the tests. Mom did not know she could. She believed the power of these tests. She believed they were mandated and had to have permission to relieve her daughter's anxiety.

Districts are actually putting five-year-young students just entering kindergarten in front of a computer with headphones on for an hour to assess them. This is their experience *before* starting school. Why are we assessing them with things we are quite clear they don't likely know yet? We know what most of these students need to learn: letter recognition, letter sounds, and common word recognition. However, we shame these vulnerable, impressionable youngsters by forcing them to attempt all these things they cannot do. They begin their educational experience thinking school is a really hard place with an "I can't" belief about themselves.

When the scores are shared, the parents of the kindergarten students gather and cautiously share the percentages of their students' correct choices, interpreting them as a ranking. The numbers hover around 60 percent and below. This is an experience of shaming students *and* their parents, as if their children are somewhat lacking before they even start school. This begins the cycle of shame that results in excessive assessments.

When I first became a principal in 1994, the letter sent home to parents explained the upcoming annual IGAP tests (Illinois Goals Achievement Program) as a "snapshot" of learning. It implied this snapshot was only one stagnant photo in the yearlong dynamic movie of visuals and descriptions of students' learning. This snapshot metaphor has turned into a gold medal, implying a race where everyone is in a competition: students, teachers, and administrators. However, it is not a selected choice race. It is mandated and causes tremendous anxiety to all those involved. Those not reaching the medal often feel less than and that is most of our population in schools—students and teachers!

Our testing system is that of entrapment. It is more about revealing what is not known than what is known. Our tests in school do not measure success, either. They do not measure how well we live our lives or how well we treat others. They do not measure what is really important in life—developing sustaining relationships that honor people for who they are and what they know and experience, not dismissing them for who they are not and what they do not know.

When I began working with Terry, I was told he was new to the school this year in eighth grade and the lowest reader in the school. He was much lower than any student in the lowest group of the reading specialist, and there was no place for him in any small group.

I learned in the first minute of our first session that he guessed at each word on the first page of *Strive* Book One. The words were tab, sad, rag, and jam. I knew he had not learned the *short a* consonant/vowel/consonant pattern well and had relied on guessing for many years, forming an ineffective habit. His guessing based on one or more consonant letters in a word was not working well for him in his reading. He stumbled, unsure of every word, confirming his lack of confidence in reading *over* and *over* again.

In our first session, we immediately entered the learning zone so he could feel success. I taught him the pattern, and how it worked with every cvc syllable he would encounter. He began to read better in that first session. In a couple of sessions, he was intentionally using the pattern recognition he had learned and confidently decoded, paying attention to all of the letters in the word. His teaching assistant and I marveled at his perseverance with the slow formation of the words on his lips. We could see in his eyes his mastery of this pattern, finally, to become a comfortable reader.

Seven weeks after beginning *Strive*, I asked Terry, "When we began working together, you were at a 1 on a scale of 1-10 because you struggled with the first four words on the first page; where do you consider yourself now?" He replied, "8."

Emotion filled me. In seven weeks, Terry had become a confident, intentional, deliberate reader of letters and syllable patterns, words, phrases, sentences, and paragraphs. The deliberate, effective reading motivated him to read, filled his self efficacy as a confident learner and turned his world around from "I can't" to "I can." And "I want to."

When I described this experience to my college students, they asked me what assessments I used. I replied that four words revealed the struggle he was having. To put him through any more assessment than that would have been much too painful, as it would have kept him in a place he lives much of the time: "I can't. I don't know." I was not going to waste one more second of his precious learning time keeping him in that place of his perceived failure and feeling shame.

Terry became the master of his learning to read. He chose what he needed to practice, set the pace, and moved on to a new skill when he felt ready. When the *Review Your Learning* page appeared at the end of each skill pattern, his eyes would open wide from a smile. The message to Terry was that we were at a celebration because he had just learned a new pattern and was ready to read them all mixed up.

As with all pages, the words on the *Review Your Learning* page are always open to more practice if the learner deems it necessary. The teaching assistant and I would also take note of patterns that might need more practice. However, Terry discerned his own need nearly always identical to our notes.

Learning to read in adolescence feels so overwhelming that it is like attempting to climb Mount Everest in flip-flops. It is actually paralyzing to even get started. Learning one thing can change the trajectory. Terry learned the very first pattern, and the second was easier than the first, and so on. Race-to-the-top mentality does not work for all learners. Very often, that mindset can make one feel worse about himself; causes one to feel that he is not enough. Measuring oneself against others can feel debilitating and result in a shutdown.

It was implementing what I knew about changing behaviors that worked for Terry. It happens one moment at a time, one minute at a time, one hour, and one day at a time. It happens when we are gentle with ourselves. It happens when we are forgiving when we are not perfect. It happens because we feel good intrinsically about what is happening to us when the change occurs. It is so gradual and infinitesimal sometimes we hardly even know it is happening.

I believe what works best is reviewing how far we have come, reveling in the accumulation of gradual moments together. Terry became a confident reader because he was successful in his new learning, which accumulated to create a new belief about himself as a reader and a learner. He measured his increased capacities, which charged the intrinsic motivation inside of him to do more.

Mihaly Csikszentmihali, in his book, *Flow: The Psychology of Optimal Experience*, describes, "Contrary to what we believe...the best moments in our lives are not the passive, receptive, relaxing times...Optimal experience is thus something *we make* happen. For a child, it could be placing with trembling fingers the last block on a tower she has built, higher than any she has built so far." (1990, p. 3)

This is what I believe about measurement. It is a personal best, one that we decide, goals that we set, and measurement we create for ourselves as learners. Teachers and coaches can guide the process to help learners reach their own goals, goals that produce a sense of personal triumph and success.

As a national education consultant, the most frequent question I hear is, "What about assessments?" In my head, it is translated, "what about the number on the scale?" I explain that when we devote more of our energy to the most effective learning processes and build learning capacities in our students, we are educating successful test takers.

When we have students asking questions and create meaning as inspired readers, engaging in conversation about text, we are truly educating with lifelong enduring value. They ask again about the end result. And they ask because that is all anyone ever asks them.

So why do we still have this fixed system? Why do we continually give our education system the power with their tests, grades, and standards? They tell us what everyone should know, how everyone should learn, what measurements will tell us that we are educated. And many of us believe them, even when we have counter evidence. We know in our hearts it isn't so.

We know there are multiple intelligences, they ebb and flow, and there is no fixed state of smartness. We let them bully us and create a system that is so unhealthy for our children, and for us, as educators. Students pull their eyebrows out at eight years old due to anxiety about the upcoming test. And we, as adults, have anxiety on a daily basis about the tests that measure our children's and our own value.

Grades are another ranking measurement that destroys the concept of enoughness. Grades help students translate themselves into not enough, almost enough, and enough (although not really fulfilling, or worse, arrogant). Grades can also cause tragedies. In one Chicago Public School, special education students cannot receive grades higher than a D. No matter what! They can receive 100 percent on their work that day, but the highest they will ever get is a D. This translates to the children, parents, and the rest of the population that they are "less than," and worse, failures.

At ages six, seven, and eight years old, the school system informs these precious, impressionable children and families that they are failures, not worth more than a D in our society. This is a travesty!

While reading a journal article on the concept of *hoarding*, I found the psychology of "excessive accumulation" compelling. I started to feel the similarities with what was happening to the accumulation of data in our schools. Phrases in the article such as "our culture of more" and the increased stress caused by acquiring too much, designed in my mind how we have become *Data Hoarders*.

The excessive data and progress monitoring has taken place of actual learning time and it puts up walls between what we think about learning and real learning. I believe educators now collect so much data they do not even know what to do with it all. (*Psychology Today*, March/April, 2012)

One statement in the article said, "owning something causes you to overestimate its worth." This speaks to our raising the value of all the data we are collecting. Furthermore, the collection of "data" becomes linked to our self-worth as educators. We have a false sense of power with this information.

Administrators, politicians, key policy makers in education have ingrained into our society, parents, and teachers that the numbers hold the value of a student's self-worth. So we keep piling on the numerical measuring that has put us in a national danger zone. The more we take up time and space with our numerical accumulation, the harder it is to get anything else done.

The healing necessary for "hoarding" is a good model for educators. It begins with the process of *divestment*—determining which data provides the greatest value, what is needed, and for what purpose. Testing speed reading over accuracy and comprehension needs to be questioned. Another strategy, one in one out = if a newer, more purposeful assessment is discovered, have it replace what is already there.

The conclusion of the article states that the divestment process is painful, however worth it, because the "tossed clutter will set you free." The new space for us in education provides space for vibrant, energetic, and sustained learning.

How can our students flourish in school and feel fulfilled as learners when all the evaluation processes tell so many of them and judge them as failures again and again and again? Who benefits from our hierarchical numerical ranking system? If we would concentrate on doing things differently, even for a while, we might see things drastically change for the better. There would be a sense of relief from the pressure cooker we are in, and in our more relaxed state, real achievement can occur. It is certainly worth our effort to try. It was refreshing to hear President Obama's state of the union address in January 2012: "To teach with creativity and passion; to stop teaching to the test; and to replace teachers who just aren't helping kids learn."

When a baby is learning to walk, the spills outnumber the successful steps (Stages of Learning, Appendix Two). The baby does not really know that the final outcome is the walking stage. They are totally motivated by the momentary success of the standing, the holding on, and taking the first step. We celebrate! We do not think for even one moment that this is not enough.

This is enough, because we know the achievement is in the standing up towards one small step. We watch the baby and revel in the approximation each time. Babies are focused on their path, not their destination. They fill their sense of worth in their efforts, their triumph of what they did that very moment, not shamed by what they yet cannot do. They have a strong sense of self efficacy and take the next step because they are in the zone of "I can!" They are not focused on how others are doing around them. They do not allow external pressures.

Often, when pushed by an adult, the baby plops themselves right down on their bottom. They set and go at their own pace. They fall and rise, both important parts of the process. And most importantly, the falls and realigning for stance are crucial for their process of regaining balance. It is NOT just about the walking. The ebb and flow of balance is what actually allows them to achieve the eventual outcome. When they enter the walking stage the youngsters hold on now and then because they seek their own guidance as they practice and become more confident walkers. We cannot find this balance for them.

Stumbling does not discourage the baby. They forge ahead because their goal is exactly what they are doing at this moment in time. Support and encouragement are ancillary to their intrinsic motivation. We can honor our students in schools with this same sense of self-monitoring. We can celebrate their learning process and individual progress and not measure against the "not yet" standard. When we celebrate the now, "Wow, look what you can do!" just like we do for babies, we feed a healthy self efficacy.

When employers are asked about the most important qualities they want in their organizations, it is not the highest test scores. A strong self efficacy is described with qualities as self starter, ability to learn new things, perseverance, confidence, ability to overcome challenges.

Employers also mention qualities such as getting along with others, able to work in a diverse environment, able to relate to cross generations.

Employers mention teamwork which is building community. They mention the ability to collaborate and build off each other's energies. They want people to work well together; create synergy. They do not mention able to work by themselves regardless of others in the organization. They might mention the ability to overcome challenges. The qualities we are nurturing in schools are not the qualities we are seeking in our places of work. There is a terrible disconnect going on.

We are starving our children of the vibrant education and learning environments we could be offering that ensure qualities for successful contributors in our society. As a principal, I do not remember what grades my students received. I do remember relationships, triumphant learning moments, learning celebrations, personalities, emotions, and behaviors.

I remember students' and teachers' hurts and joys. I remember when a student was so grateful to have a friend on the first day of school. I remember the myriad of occasions when teachers sent students down to my office to share with me their joy of learning or grab my hand to see learning in their classrooms.

I remember a teaching assistant, with tears in her eyes, because Richard was excited about writing for the first time in his life. Richard had been a struggling student in school (special education), and was not able to do any of the curricula in his grades. He had a parallel program, so he would be with his peers, but not do anything they were doing.

When we transformed the writing program in my school, Richard had composed a story about his dog, and it brought tears to all of us. Richard had not ever written anything of importance to himself. He had not written much but one-word answers before, usually to a question the teacher asked. He was in sixth grade.

I remember when my students and teachers felt successful as learners, or not. And I remember most of the relationships formed with my students and teachers. I remember the powerful conversations we had surrounding learning. I remember Friday reading and writing roundtables, where we shared what was working in our classrooms and what were our struggles.

I remember the teachers and myself as learners in a community of learning. Not knowing was our challenge and celebration together as we figured it out. Our learning process and progress were honored, as a group, as we valued each other's contributions.

I remember one Friday roundtable, where someone suggested we split up in primary and intermediate groups. A sixth-grade teacher responded emphatically, "No!" and showed us a clipboard he had developed for keeping track of the writing conferences he had with students and the conversations about their writing. He shared that this idea was inspired by the kindergarten teacher. We shared and our challenges became fertile ground for our individual and collective growing.

I remember the yearbook photographer sharing how much he loved to photograph in my school. Everyone was happy. He could walk in any classroom, the lunchroom, teachers' lounge, and feel welcomed, not intruding on secrets he felt in so many other schools. He commented at my school, "Everyone is always smiling." They lit up his camera.

We want our students to be educated, informed, to acquire skills, knowledge, and experience. Do they ever get to decide what they get to be informed about or what skills they will acquire? Are students who test well the most successful in life? Do we have a correlation with high test scores in third grade, fifth grade, eighth grade, or high school with healthy life success?

Success

How do we measure success without shaming?

Success is determined on an individual basis. When we are able to define our own success, we are more often harder on ourselves than others. We are more often motivated to do well because shame is not standing in our way. Why was Terry successful in learning how to read after all these years? He was in good schools; in fact, schools with great reputations. Yet the system had failed him.

In a few weeks with *Strive*, Terry was experiencing success in his reading without comprehensive assessments, progress monitoring, elaborate schematics, a teacher pacing guide, and without elaborate teacher instructions. Less had resulted in more. It took Terry, me, his teaching assistant, and reading skills.

Success happened because Terry felt empowered and believed he could for the first time because he was learning, one small moment at a time, building the cumulative successes into long-lasting habit changing. It started with creating a trusting relationship.

Immediately, Terry learned a pattern that worked in many instances because our brains seek and access patterns more easily than random locating. He determined what he felt confident doing and what he needed to practice, and the new habits quickly replaced the older, slower, ineffective behavior of guessing. Each successful learning moment strengthened to solidify previous learning.

Each session was maintained in Terry's *learning zone*. His teaching assistant would tell me frequently how he looked forward to our sessions. I believed Terry felt successful with me, safe as a struggling learner—an unfamiliar feeling in his other classes. He felt special and successful as a learner in our relationship. He mattered.

In each session, Terry started with review of what he knew well, moved on to learning something new, and always ending with a feeling of fulfilling learning and reading well. We maintained Vygotsky's "zone of proximal development," not too hard and not too easy, just right. Terry began to read on his own with greater facile, therefore feeling successful and motivated to do more.

During one school week, after two days of challenging his teaching assistant in working with her, he told me on day three, "I just want to read." His behavior was a reminder to us to listen to our students. So we added sessions that were exclusively reading. Reading was safe for him now; he felt successful, rather than ashamed. A whole world was opening up to him through reading, and he liked how it felt.

We have this illusion that success is a number on a test score. In reality, test scores are not the final outcome at all. Success is our own feeling of achievement. Test scores are temporary. They give us very little, if any, information about our students' learning. In most conversations with educators, testing is our enemy. Instead of helping us and informing us, they punish us.

For example, when we weigh ourselves on a scale, the numbers do not tell us anything we need to do differently for our health. Our bodies tell us and so do our feelings. If we concentrate on doing differently, creating new habits, even for a while, we might see things drastically change for the better.

Peter Johnston tells us, "In productive classrooms, teachers don't just teach children skills: they build emotionally and relationally healthy learning communities. Teachers create intellectual environments that produce not only technically competent students, but also caring, secure, actively literate human beings." (2004, Johnston, *Choice Words*) Peter describes success as productive classrooms.

However, the changes we know we need to make are not often the ones we make. For example, every educator on the planet would agree that more engagement by students is a good thing. Nevertheless, most school changes result in less engagement and more adult control. Engagement and compliance do not work well together. Compliance means someone else's control, usually the teachers. Engagement and empowerment work well together. When we allow students to make decisions about their learning, we develop their integrity as learners.

For our students, their learning has to be enough. Actually, it is what really matters the most. Success is about *enoughness*. How do we obtain *enoughness*? We do it by NOT focusing all of our energies on the future state of something. That keeps us stuck. That keeps us in a state of "not enough" and of "I can't" rather than "I can." All the preparation, pretesting, diagnosing, progress monitoring, local assessments, and state and national assessments have replaced valuable learning time.

Finding enough is a hard thing to do because every single stage and all the outside voices tell us just the opposite. We are constantly being told we are not enough. We are not reading fast enough, well enough, at a high enough level.

How do we ever know Enough when the world tells us the opposite?

It is time we declare *Enough* for ourselves (Louden). It is time to declare that not only are we enough, but we will be telling you when it is enough, not the other way around. Our personal learning zone is the optimal learning stage. Learning ebbs and flows and it works best when we find our zone of enoughness. This is a place where we feel good about who we are and our learning now, at this point in time. We are okay at this very moment. It does not mean that we do not have the desire to improve or know and learn more. What it means is that we declare satisfaction at the very moment in time so we can smile to ourselves, and feel satisfied. We can declare: we are enough! This is what motivates us to do *more*.

With *Strive*, students make all the decisions about their learning basic reading skills. They determine what they know and what they need to practice. They decide when and how often they will practice. They decide when they feel ready for the teacher to listen to them when they review learned patterns.

For the first time in their lives, these struggling readers are taking the power to help themselves become better readers. These learners are taking charge and investing in their learning in a way they have not had the opportunity to do before. Their investment determines their return. They are not doing it *for* the teacher. They are doing it *for* themselves. *Strive* creates an "I can" (often for the first time ever) in students' self-talk about themselves as readers.

When I decided it was time to eat healthy because my health was compromised by too much weight, I had a decision to make. I could follow the latest and greatest diet to lose weight quickly. Or, I could find a plan that offered me health and still gave me plenty to eat, the ability to eat my favorite foods, and flexibility to eat out at restaurants.

A starvation diet is usually temporary and I needed to create a style of living that would be sustained. Long term required me to form new healthy, sustainable habits, replacing the ineffective ones. Stepping on a scale for measurement of success was an ineffective habit I abandoned.

When we desire to make lasting habit formation, we need to be intentional about it. First, we need to bring it to our awareness that something has to change. When we think about it at our most vivid consciousness, we can think about replacing it with the new thing.

For example, my university students would share their students first' response to anything new was, *I can't*. This was a habit that was not effective for their learning because it formed a barrier. The teachers helped them replace it with a new habit that was more effective. Beginning lessons with familiar tasks or knowledge the students shifted from their typical response of *I can't* to *I can*. The power of this positive self talk was more effective for their new learning.

Another ineffective habit struggling students use in reading is guessing at words. Since most syllables fit in a pattern, there is no need to guess. When students learn these patterns well, they replace the ineffective habit of guessing with accessing the syllable patterns in their brains, creating more facile reading. This easier, systematic acquisition of syllable patterns offers students a more effective habit, replacing one that has caused them struggle in reading, often, for years.

In our attempt to do better, we often create new controls that impede learning rather than assist. For example, our elaborate assessments that cause shame in students exasperates the feelings of *I can't* on a frequent basis. Forcing students to take tests that shame them are unnecessary and damaging. Another practice, out of desperation to teach reading, is increasing the list of sight words for students to memorize. Sight words on many lists fit nicely into the patterns we teach, and these words do NOT need to be memorized.

We often choose the starvation diet in schools by following the latest and greatest curriculum panacea, the silver bullet, at the cost of starving our children, in the illusion of the final outcome: Higher test scores? Getting into the top colleges? Or are we seeking to educate our children, to give them academic, social, and emotional health to live fully as an inspired learner, to honor those individuals that come through our school doors and value each others' contributions in life no matter what endeavor they choose? What if we sought to create a confidence about learning, and enoughness, and squelch the feeling of never enough, for learners to have a strong self efficacy about themselves as a learner in anything they encounter.

If we want our learners to get from the place of "I wonder" to "I now know," and "I now can do," we do this by cultivating enoughness, not by cultivating "never enough," which is what we do now. Never enough leaves us feeling empty. It leaves us feeling void, only to desire what we do not have, and not embracing what we do. Never enough keeps us in a comparative state with others, a feeling of never measuring up, lacking rather than filling. Enoughness is the opposite- a feeling of fulfilled, gratitude, motivation for more of this feeling.

How do we guide students to determine their Enough learning?

We inspire and guide students to answer these questions for themselves:

What will I learn?
How much will I learn?
When will I learn?
How will I know when I am learning? And how will I know when I am not learning?
What will learning look like when not planned?

When we shift the celebration to the following:
This day I will read and write, learn new things, discuss things with other students so our learning expands with each other's thinking.

At the end of the day, it is measurably a great day! These accumulate 1+1+1+1=4 really good fulfilling learning days.

Do I allow the time to produce the outcome that will surely come with doing the best things every day for a healthy education? By lessening the anxiety and frustration for students and teachers, we can all be free to teach and learn. We can be free to go deeper in text rather than study exclusively for tests they will take, only to be forgotten because these test items are superficial learning. Studying items for a test is a diet of processed foods. It bulks us of empty nutrition, filling time and space where real learning could occur.

A friend of mine, an outstanding veteran teacher, called me in a panic at the start of a school year, in her third decade of teaching. "The new reading curriculum requires forty pages of instruction in the teacher's guide for ONE daily lesson." She could not think of anything else. She could not concentrate on getting to know her new students for the year. She was fraught with anxiety. This teacher had been a very successful teacher of reading for many years.

Now she felt inadequate. Now she felt if she did not read and follow the forty pages of instruction, her lesson would not be enough. This is a travesty! This veteran teacher had been successfully teaching reading for years. Now she was feeling shame and doubting her abilities in meeting the needs of her students, and in addition, causing high anxiety. This teacher, after thirty-plus years of developing master teaching pedagogy, was shamed and placed in the zone of *I can't* rather than *I can.*

To illustrate with another health metaphor in our society: We are overweight and compromising our health at an alarming rate. Yet, we have the most scientifically, well-researched, fastest, best, quickest ways to lose weight than ever in history. How is this possible? It is because we are measuring the wrong thing.

We are focusing on the outcome. Every day, we get on the scale only to feel disappointed and frustrated. So we lose hope, lose motivation. And we look for the next, best, latest diet that will create the outcome we seek without doing the real, sustaining work that needs to be done. And we know the intentional, healthy work that changes habits forever.

This is what we are doing in education. We are starving our children of a comprehensive, vibrant, vigorous education. By concentrating on a reductionistic, narrow curriculum, mainly, that which is tested, we are creating educational poverty and have been increasingly creating this poverty for almost two decades. We know that success requires more than the ability to take tests, yet that is all we seem to care about in schools, and revere testing as the end all, be all.

Our current curriculum programs offered by most publishing conglomerates look like grand buffets of food filled with an overabundance of unhealthy items. One needs to discern what is best, what is healthy. However, people are gluttonous at buffets because it is there. We are also gluttonous with curriculum. There are many things that should not be eaten, just like there is only so much time in the day and many things in the curriculum are not healthy for students.

Educators get so confused; they know in their hearts what is a healthy curriculum, what healthy learning looks and feels like, but there are so many outside sources telling them otherwise that they begin to believe them.

How do we know what should be done and what should not be done?

The same way we know what should be eaten and what should not be eaten.

When we concentrate on healthy teaching pedagogy we quickly observe what works best for our learners. We also know to eliminate what is not healthy and not working. The more customization of learning that occurs for our students, the more effective and enduring of achievement. When we stay away from the most processed curriculum, greater learning ensues just like when we stay away from the most processed foods for a healthier body. Forty pages of instructions for one day's reading lesson is like the finest white flour, processed everything healthy out of it.

What works best?

- Offering less, not more
- Allowing empowerment of learning
- Less teacher planning and control
- Choice of text, content
- Choice of expression, poetry, paper
- Choice of practice

Less is more effective. Yet we constantly create gluttony; we do more and more and students learn less and less. We can no longer allow these buffets into our schools and give the power to the conglomerate publishing companies that are creating GLUTTONY. We are drowning in a mess!

My niece, an aspiring teacher, contacted me to send her a few of my father's letters. She was to write about a person who was influential and someone she did not know very well. She considered these letters as primary sources. Written to me when I went away to college in the fall of 1971, I have cherished these letters throughout my life. They are my father's Voice- depicting his personality, humor, challenges as he shared himself with my during my first absence from home. Tory emailed me, "These letters are really amazing to read- they give me such a vibrant image of who your father was, my grandfather, and I really wish I had been able to get to know him." His words speak volumes about who he was as a person, what mattered to him that could not be captured in any photo of him. This is a primary source letter I sent Tory.

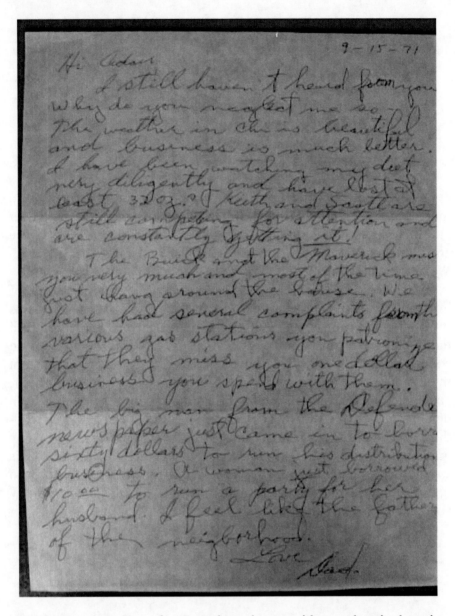

I hope when Tory is a teacher she provides authentic learning experiences of understanding self content as she was offered in her university course.

Measurement by tests is strangling us. We have this dark cloud called *Testing* that hovers over educators and students every moment in school that whispers, "if it is on the test it is important, if not, unnecessary." I am not advocating for a lack of measurement. It is crucial we know how we are growing. However, students could be measuring themselves. Have they engaged in reading, writing, sharing in conversation about text, writing from text that inspires them, or from what someone has said? That could be our measure, not a single numerical score that says we have read all these words correctly and at a fast rate.

I had asked one of my young students to read comfortably fast and accurately. He responded, "My teacher makes me go fast but I am not accurate." How has fast become more important than accuracy? By only looking at a single numeric outcome, we are missing those opportunities to celebrate real learning.

Real learning is about creating habits that feed us healthy amounts of knowledge and understanding, keeps us in our learning zone, and is customized for everyone. Vygotsky described the "zone of proximal development"; I call it the *Goldilocks* theory because it explains the concept of just right, the zone of enough.

When learning is too difficult, we can feel overwhelmed, even shut down, and learning gets stuck. When learning is too easy, we are not taking anything in that is new, so we are not really learning. The zone of proximal development gets this learning just right. It is learning that is not too difficult that we attempt to avoid it. It is learning where we do not feel overwhelmed. In fact, it revitalizes us; it makes us feel so alive. We know "we can." Not all learning is in the just right zone.

When students get a taste of success in their learning zone, they want more. When they feel their efforts are enough and they feel good about what they achieve, they want more, especially when they have passed through a great challenge for themselves. They pass through their own threshold of success. It is different for each one of us. Some people learn faster than others.

The great thing about *Enough* is that it can occur at any point in time; each learner has a personal experience. Since it is not decided by any outside source or person or any point in time, it can actually happen quicker or slower, depending on circumstances. Educators make assumptions about what works and what does not work in our schools. Often, these assumptions are based on our own experiences and self as learners.

Teachers are often good students. Teachers often have had good experiences as learners in school. They feel safe in the school environment. Some of our students do not feel this way and we are able to create an environment where they thrive socially, emotionally, and academically. All three feed off each other. Often, a lack in one compromises the other.

In today's schools teachers enter their schools and classrooms every single day with an anxiety that they are not doing enough. Not doing enough for their students, the parents of their students, and not doing enough for their administrators. And certainly not doing enough for themselves, often relegating themselves to the very last with nothing left over, always feeling depleted.

How can we turn this around?

What are the possibilities?

How do we do enough for our students?

First, we can shorten the time frame of enoughness. Rather than determine the expectation of an outcome at a future date, how about we create an achievable outcome for today? What if the class determines together what is a good amount of time for their reading and sharing? By empowering students with decisions, we give them a sense of their own accountability. How about if we read for thirty minutes? That is achievable. It is not a certain amount of pages, or even a certain amount of chapters. But it is a time amount that is achievable in the classroom by each learner.

How about if we make our enoughness about what we *do* rather than a fixed, future state such as a score? How about if we guide our students to determine their enoughness individually? What does it look like for teachers to be doing enough in the classroom? How can enough be measured? Is there a standard for enough? Or is enough customized for each lesson and each student?

If we go back to our food metaphor, how do we know when we are full and satisfied? We know because we feel satiated. We know because we are no longer hungry. Have we learned things, have we been able to ask questions and answer them? Do we still have things we are wondering about? Curriculum programs are created to keep teachers on track within a certain subject area domain. There is a lesson structure, content, and pacing.

Do these always work? Every group of students is very different. Customization in lessons offer increased individual achievement. When teachers ask themselves learner based questions, answers are revealing: Are my lessons engaging for each student? Are students intrigued in what we are doing in the classroom? Am I intrigued in my work? What am I doing in the classroom that sustains the greatest interest for each learner? How do I make sure students are in their zones of proximal development?

The beauty of an *Ubuntu* classroom is the teacher is not solely responsible for answering these questions. The students become involved in making these decisions. The teachers ask themselves continually: How do I create the environment so my students take charge of their own learning? How do I empower them as lifelong learners? When these questions are shared, there is a great sense of relief in the learning environment. The solutions become *we*, rather than I.

While studying the common core standards for our nation, I thought about how important "evidence" is for us as educators, and for our students to use in their learning development. After fourteen weeks working with Terry, I asked his teacher to inform me of his reading behaviors with her.

She listed the following improvements as evidence:

- Willingness to participate in reading activities
- Feels successful about the time he spends with you
- Feels more confident
- Works to sound out words
- Discusses the meaning of words
- Has come to class and tells us about new words he has learned

- Increase in his ability to decode vowel sounds and combinations
- Verbally decodes with a decreased amount of prompting
- Continues to use his strength as an audio learner when we work on stories and novels in class

As I reveled in the "success" Terry was experiencing, the final statement was a powerful message about the formal assessments used to progress monitor. The teacher said that the AIMSweb – Maze scores have not been consistent. Bravo! Terry, as a newly confident, capable, successful reader was not going to let any assessment or progress monitoring get in the way of his learning and shame him anymore!

Finally

Rather than quantitative data, the popular "research says," I chose instead to tell my stories from my knowledge and experiences to illustrate my beliefs about education. Consciously avoiding the scientific use of wide data allowed me to provide a more customized view of learning from my own experiences and focusing on well known subjects: myself, my children, my students, my colleagues.

I also shared others' words I have internalized over the years that resonate with my beliefs and experiences. There is an abundance of wide data out there. Many education books follow a similar format and include this wide data. I think sometimes we follow the wide data because we think we should. We hear this is working elsewhere, yet inside ourselves, we experience otherwise. *Enough* is providing a different way of looking at what is possible by looking differently at what we have seen.

For my entire life, I craved feeling included, as many of us do, and learned early on to create relationships that honored those around me. I now know the word that describes this: *Ubuntu* is collective energy—it is needing others to be who we are because we are full, not because we are empty. I always thought that my wanting to be like others was a bad thing, that somehow, I was not enough. It is the opposite. By finding in others what is about me is actually finding myself and finding that others matter, too. It is finding that I am enough.

In discovering about others, I find who they are and how they matter to me; how I can continually learn about and from them, and find the importance and enoughness in them. It is a sense of feeling connected rather than disconnected. *Ubuntu* is created with each individual we encounter when we value them in our lives, rather than judge and criticize them. I was learning about learning and humanness from Terry as he was learning to read.

We all struggle with feelings of inadequacies and enoughness. At times, it is more severe than others, but we feel it. Whether we believe it ourselves, or whether it is the message we hear from others, it is there. We are able to change the tape for ourselves. We are also able to help our learners change their tapes so they believe in themselves.

When we believe we are enough, for ourselves and for others, we feel full and the only way we can accumulate our feeling of success. Just imagine if we boycotted the system that is creating this travesty of "not enough" for so many of our students and ourselves! These measures of inadequacy are bred in our society by the assessments we assign for our children throughout their schooling.

Brene' Brown's research teaches us that we are wired neurobiologically for connections; it is what gives us purpose. She also espouses through her study of thousands of stories over many years that our ability to connect is directly related to our belief that we are worthy. We must create this belief in our children in schools. Our greatest lesson to our students is to develop this strong sense of worthiness by creating an environment where they are *enough*.

As we emerge into adulthood and older adulthood, we still need what we needed in our childhood. We continue to form our identity by having some control over our lives. We also form our identity by connecting with others to deepen relationships through our stories and shared experiences. We need to continue to matter.

When we have a Voice, a say in our lives, we feel agency and competent. We need to work diligently at believing in ourselves because so much of our world tells us we are not good enough, and we believe that instead. We allow others to measure our worth of ourselves. The world tells us we need higher test scores, faster this, bigger that, and race to the top of where are we going? We have created a culture of more as an illusion of better.

We do not celebrate what we have accomplished because we negate it by stating the part we haven't done yet. It is a tragedy! We take enough and make it a not-enough statement. And we believe it. We tell a child he has improved in his reading, and then show him how much further he has to go. It is counterproductive. We must celebrate our small, often infinitesimal successes, even our approximations. The accumulation is the success. The final outcome is often anticlimactic. The final product does not bring the joy the actual learning process creates.

After two months in the process of Terry in his learning zone, he asked me how many *Strive* books were left. I was quite sure I had told him, but realized in his question that he was not ready to hear it in the beginning. Learning the pattern on the first page was enough for him. He could not take in all there was yet to do. However, after feeling success with the first book and well into the second, he wanted to know. He could handle what was left; he could view himself as almost done with only one book remaining.

We are punishing our children every single day by not accepting them as enough and creating an environment where they feel inadequate. They feel this because teachers feel this way as well and it permeates the environment they create from their own feelings. We shame children every day. We are always apologizing for not being enough. Children also use these words and their feelings of not enoughness show up in their faces and behaviors.

We now know, though, in our tumultuous world, especially of late, that best, faster, fastest, most is not an assurance of anything extrinsic, and most definitely not intrinsic. When we become the most caring, compassionate selves possible, we have achieved success, where we honor others and value contributions of each individual; we feel the most fulfilled.

When we focus on ways of feeling filled and worthy, we then treat others as worthy. Our own feeling of worthiness allows us to treat others with caring, compassion, and empathy. Each behavior towards others with these social and emotional capacities spreads to benefit society as a whole. These positive behaviors become contagious and epitomize caring learning communities and social justice.

We have this illusion that the future will bring us where we want to be. The irony is that by living in that future, it actually robs us of the gift of the moment. The reality is that the now is where we want to be, and if we create a NOW that is healthy, inspiring, joyful, then we learn how to replicate that.

By living in the future, we suffer from not enoughism—not faster, not enough this and that—which keeps us frustrated, feeling less than, rather than enough, rather than being able to focus on "I am enough." The "I am not enough" feels defeating and is not motivating.

In reality, it is the "I am enough" that is our greatest motivator, because we want more of that feeling. Success is being enough and enough is today, at this moment. It is the end of a filling moment, the end of reading a passage that moves us, that compels us to discuss with someone else. It is the end of the reading of a word-syllable pattern where we previously struggled. It is sharing our story and knowing we matter to someone else. Success is very personal. It is not determined by any system, any outside source. It is determined within each one of us. And we must declare "we are enough!" This is our success!

We spend so much time in what is not working well we do not even realize it. It becomes our comfort zone, yet we feel the discomfort every day. Then when we have an experience where something works better, we realize the not-working state more clearly. But the not-working state is all we know. Yet, the new experience makes us feel so alive; we revel in the experience and wonder how to get more.

For example, a teacher who feels downtrodden with a lockstep robotic curriculum finds a new way and her students respond with an energy and engagement she has not seen before. She wants more of this engagement and so do her students.

If we are totally real and honest about the current state of most schools, we can admit our children are starving, and so are we. We can shift to educational nourishment; what feeds us in a healthy and fulfilling way, not what starves us. Our hearts tell us what we are doing is not really working. It is on the students' faces when they scream to us through their eyes, "Please, not one more test! Just let me learn please, just let me learn!"

We have the possibility to create for our children what we want for our own selves as adults.

We want to feel enough.

We also want to fit in, not feel like an outcast.

We want to feel included and include others.

We want to feel honored by others and to honor others.

We want to matter to others, and we want others to matter to us.

We want to stop feeling less than as measured by others' standards, and pictures of us.

We want to stop being judged by others as how they define themselves. We rather want to be honored for who *we* are. This happens with authentic, intentional connection opportunities that develops optimal relational rapport. Understanding replaces judgment; expectations of behavior become caring guidance as a natural part of personal growth. Building on *enough* increases motivation, rather than causing blame, feelings of inferiority and discouragement.

Improving the quality of our schools means improving the quality of the experience for our children on a daily basis. When they are engaged, inspired learners who wonder and learn to navigate their own learning, understand their growth process, they feel enough in their everyday experiences.

We can create joy in our classrooms and schools. We do not want our teachers to have to close the doors for first-grade students to celebrate a holiday. We do not want them to experience anxiety in rushing, doing, replacing the joy of learning with rigorous, stifling curriculum.

Imagine if we had a seismic revolution in education to create enough, right now. The good news—in fact, great news—is that we can turn this around rather quickly. Just like with food, it can take a few weeks for our bodies to celebrate optimal nutrition when we eliminate or even lessen the processed, unhealthy foods we eat. It celebrates with more energy, less stuffed feel, even happier and more joyful attitude. When we feed our children healthy, invigorating, honoring curriculum we will soon end the poverty of learning in our schools.

My dream is to do this right now!

There are risks and costs to a program of action. But they are far less than the long-range risks of comfortable inaction.

—John F. Kennedy (1917-1963) —

Appendix One
The New 3 R's of Learning

Relationships = Creating a mutual learning zone; teacher learns from the student in knowing best how to guide them and sustain their learning progress. Creating caring relationships among students with each other is revered as a primary purpose in classrooms, schools, and with our home communities.

Regency = Learners exercise the power in their learning; raising their self efficacy in all learning.

Real Learning = Authentic materials for learning to support students' self content and to provide choices for expanding their world of literacy in all content areas.

HOW

Relationships = Honoring self content as the most valuable to seed other learning. Caring about what learners bring with them in knowledge, experience, and interests to spark the content of the world. This is the key to tapping into intrinsic motivation. When learners feel honored, they are present with full intrinsic engagement. Relationships are intentionally developed among all the students in each classroom, between classrooms, and in the school by providing social and emotional opportunities throughout the school day to foster a caring learning environment.

Guiding a student who is struggling in acquiring basic reading skills requires a mutual caring relationship for optimal student learning. The teacher listens carefully to understand the learners to guide them, honoring their self content, customizing learning ways and materials. (For example, a learner who loves humor benefits from practicing skill patterns in silly sentences. A learner who loves to draw benefits from practicing skill patterns in text they illustrate.)

Regency = Fostering empowerment for learners to navigate their own learning. The teacher serves as a guide, cheerleader, and mentor allowing students to make decisions about their own learning, interests, conversation, and pacing.

When learners are empowered in their learning and assessment of self they develop a healthy self efficacy. For example, in writing, students make choices about the content. They choose formats among the many shared in the classroom. They may write letters to important people in their life. Their confidence as writers grows with each experience.

Real learning = Authentic materials of the world are used for content. Students, adults, and a variety of sources inspire learning substance.

Learning unfolds in a natural, organic, dynamic manner with student wondering at the center. Humans are inherently bursting with questions and wondering about their world. Literacy comprehension expands through symbols, text, listening, viewing, and processing with others in conversation.

Elaborate teacher instructions or extensive lesson plans are unnecessary. When curriculum is primarily a set of instructions, reading and writing for others, answering questions of others, compliant students become passive vessels. Others shut down with this *Simon Says* type of teaching.

For example, students choose to investigate a topic they wonder about, find resources, collect data and share their new learning. Learners' wondering leads their searching, not prepared questions. Learners do not depend on an outside source such as teacher, assessment, or program to provide evidence of their progress. They are able to assess themselves to know how they are achieving based on what they knew in the beginning.

Appendix Two
Stages of Learning

1) <u>Starter Learning.</u> In the beginning stage, efforts are usually clumsy, awkward, and uncomfortable, like first learning to ride a bicycle. There may be many starts and stops. Observing others do what you want to do often feels overwhelming and you wonder, *How will I ever be able to do this?* I learned how to ski in my thirties. I did a week-long tap workshop in my fifties. This was the question I asked myself in both cases.

2) <u>Practice Learning.</u> As you practice what you are learning, you progress to a more refined level. Your efforts become smoother and more even. You can stay on the bicycle for longer periods of time. At this stage, you get into a rhythm and you become more comfortable. You begin to think, *I think I can do this.* As I learned and trained, and practiced in my tap workshop, I remember when I began to "think" I could just because I really wanted to.

(In order to move to the next, more comfortable, confident Progressive Learning stage, you must be compassionate with yourself and intentional for your development to be fulfilled. Intentional means answering this question: What small action am I willing to take every day (or most days) to obtain the progress I seek?

3) <u>Progressive Learning.</u> At this stage, you are pleased with the results of the efforts of your continued practice. You now know what works well for you and what doesn't. You feel a certain comfort level, which leads you to think, *I know I can do this.* This is a wonderful feeling. My starter learning just got easier. My stamina built and my "think" began to feel like "know."

4) <u>Ingrained Learning</u>. At this stage, your knowing "how to do" becomes ingrained. You attempt more complicated unknowns because the starter stage has become automatic. You begin to think, *I can't believe I thought this was hard.* I now can ski and I now can tap three hours a day, and just want to do more!

The amount of time each individual stays at each stage is personal. It depends on your time commitment, your acceptance of approximation, and your willingness to stick with it until you get to the next stage.

Appendix Three
Capacities of Literacy Comprehension

(Adapted from the *Capacities for Imaginative Learning,*
Lincoln Center for the Performing Arts, Inc., New York City)

Decoding/ Encoding: To recognize, access, understand, and express using the symbols and complex set of abilities of varying content areas. This includes, for example, letters, numbers, words, phrases, sentences, body language, and social interactions

Noticing Deeply: To identify and articulate layers of detail in (literature, art, science, music, self, and relationships, etc.) through continuous interactions over time

Embodying: To experience a work of (literature, art, relationships, etc.) through your senses, as well as emotionally and also physically (in conversation and/or written) to represent that experience

Wondering: To ask questions throughout your explorations that further your own learning (for clarification and deepening understanding); to ask divergent questions such as "What if?" and "Why?"

Making Connections: To connect what you notice and the patterns to your prior knowledge and experiences, as well as to others' knowledge and experiences, including text and multimedia resources

Identifying Patterns: To find relationships among details you notice, group them, and recognize and create patterns

Exhibiting Empathy: To honor the diverse perspectives of others in our community; to understand the experiences of others emotionally as well as thought

<u>Creating Meaning:</u> To create your own interpretations based on the previous capacities, see these in the light of others in the community, create synthesis, and express in your own voice

<u>Taking Action:</u> To act on the synthesis of what you have learned in your explorations through specific action and expression. This includes conversation, writing, the arts, as well as other realms. For example, a play written and produced, designing and planting a community garden, guiding those in a conflict with an effective problem-solving opportunity—all portray literacy comprehension in with action.

<u>Reflecting/Assessing:</u> To look back on your learning, continually assess what you have learned, assess/identify what challenges remain, and assess/identify what further learning needs to happen. This occurs not only at the end of a learning experience, but as part of what happens throughout that experience. At the end of your learning experience is also a part of beginning to learn something else!

When we speak of content areas, we typically think of a body of knowledge/skills outside of ourselves. Literacy encompasses the intellectual processes of gaining and creating meaning from outside sources, entwined with our self-content. These Learning Capacities also apply to our self-content, that which is inside of us and uniquely ours. When we honor our self-content and weave it with our new learning we develop our greatest Learning Capacities!

Literacy is primarily something people DO: it is an activity, located in the space between thought and text. Literacy does not reside in people's heads as a set of skills to be learned, and it does not just reside on paper captured in texts to be analyzed. Like all human activity, literacy is essentially social, and it is located in the interaction between people.

—Barton and Hamilton (1998) —

My Influences

I am grateful to these influences in my life who taught me among many others:

Chimamanda Adichie: The danger of a single story | Video on TED ...

www.ted.com/.../chimamanda_adichie_the_da...Oct 7, 2009 - 19 min

Tom Bird - (the book whisperer), who helped birth the book that was already inside me

Brené Brown: The power of vulnerability | Video on TED.com

www.ted.com/.../brene_brown_on_vulnerabil...Dec 23, 2010 - 20 min

Brené Brown studies human connection – our ability to empathize, belong, love. In a ...

Brene' Brown – who studies the human connection, shame resilience, and I am enough. It is the last image on Brene's TedTalk that inspired the title of this book.

Barb Cataldo – who honors the children at all costs!

Mihaly Csikszentmihalyi – Flow is being and doing where time suspends and we are lost in the space of thought and heart, and whatever action we are doing

John Dewey – Constructivist Learning, that which matters most

Paolo Freire – Critical Theory

Daniel Goleman – Social Emotional Learning and relational rapport

Sherry Jablonski – who coached me, embraced my approximations, and guided me to find enough in myself and enough in others

Peter Johnston – power of words with each other

Ellin Keene – creating understanding and joy with text

Pippi Longstocking – living an adventure

Jen Louden – Conditions of Enoughness and declaring satisfaction

Nelson Mandela – *Ubuntu*

Carol McCloud – *Have You Filled a Bucket Today? A Guide to Daily Happiness for Kids* (Ferne Press, 2006)

Jamie McKenzie – Purposeful wandering…where questioning and wondering are at the heart of all learning

Elizabeth Moje – who listens first and honors students and scholarship

Liz Murray – who shares her poignant story of becoming educated in *Breaking Night* (Hyperion, 2011)

Nietzsche – questioning of truth

Daniel Manus Pinkwater – I am living *The Big Orange Splot* (Scholastic, 1977) – My work is me and I am it, it looks like all my dreams

Plato – schooling synonymous with life

Ramajon – who helped navigate my book to the places it needed to go

Eric Schaps – Caring School Community ^{TM}

David Serpas – who continues to work with challenges to become his best

Greg Serpas – who is learning lessons in his third decade that I am learning in my sixth

Terry Jo Smith – my mentor, who listened to me, pushed me, inspired me, and taught me to view my work and my life through a critical lens

South Side Babes – my childhood friends who came back into my life after 45 years to help me know again the child I was

Vygotsky – zone of proximal development

In all affairs it's a healthy thing now and then to hang a question mark on things you have long taken for granted.
—Bertrand Russell (1872-1970) —

CPSIA information can be obtained at www.ICGtesting.com
Printed in the USA
LVOW131059220413

330297LV00001B/28/P